104 MORE ROSIE THE RIVETER STORIES

104 MORE ROSIE THE RIVETER STORIES

*Stories of working women
from World War II
as written by the Rosies themselves*

**American
Rosie the Riveter
Association®**

Published in the United States of America by the
American Rosie the Riveter Association®

Editor: Nell Carter Branum
Production Assistant: Lucy Case Lewis

Copyright © 2005 by the American Rosie the Riveter Association®
Fifth Printing 2012

Library of Congress Control Number: 2005937800
ISBN: 0976926016
       9780976926016

The front cover highlights the "We Can Do It!" picture that was created by graphic artist J. Howard Miller during World War II as a recruiting poster for Westinghouse Corporation. The poster was commissioned by the War Production Coordinating Committee, and, through the years, has come to represent all women whose work on the home front contributed to the war effort during World War II. The poster has been incorporated into the cover artwork by Daniel Branum, a Rivet member of the American Rosie the Riveter Association®.

All rights reserved. No part of this work may be reproduced in any form by any means—graphic, electronic, or mechanical—including photocopying, recording, or any process (except for brief quotations in printed interviews or by reviewers, who may quote brief passages to be printed in newspapers or magazines), without prior written permission of the American Rosie the Riveter Association®. Exception: Each author is granted permission to reproduce her own story and the title page.

American Rosie the Riveter Association®
www.rosietheriveter.net

DEDICATION

To all the women whose work during World War II contributed to the war effort, whether through the work force or through volunteer efforts. Your strength, dignity, and loyalty are still an inspiration.

PREFACE

When the American Rosie the Riveter Association® was founded on December 7, 1998, wheels were set in motion to accomplish several purposes.

First, to locate those women who had contributed to the World War II effort, either through the work force or through volunteer work, and their female descendants. Since no master list was kept during or after the war, this has required consistent one-on-one contact. The search still continues. Many Rosies are now deceased, but their daughters, granddaughters, and other family members have joined the organization for them posthumously, and have also become members themselves. More information about how to join ARRA is on page 213.

Second, to organize chapter meetings in cities across America, so that Rosies and their family members could gather for fellowship with each other. In addition, an annual national convention/reunion has been held each year in June. Rosies are encouraged to share their stories with schools and civic organizations in their hometowns, as well.

Third, to develop a Web site that connects ARRA members with other information about World War II, and perhaps even more significantly, connects today's students with information about Rosies and World War II.

And fourth, to collect the stories of as many Rosies as possible, so that the legacy of these strong and dedicated women will live on. The book you now hold in your hand is the third book of stories that the organization has published. For more information about the others, see page 214.

The contribution that these patriotic women made not only to the war effort, but ultimately to the American freedoms that we enjoy today, cannot be overstated. One combat veteran of World War II puts it this way: "What made the difference in America's triumph over her enemies during the war? We were trained for success, but so were they. We were dedicated, but so were they — it's hard to beat the dedication of a Kamikaze pilot. An important difference was that the enemy, especially in Europe, could not maintain their production of war materials because of the massive destruction by our bombers. When we shot an airplane out of the skies or killed a tank, they couldn't replace it. But with the Allies, it was a different story, because in America the factories kept running at full force, even though most able-bodied men had been called to military service. We had factories back on the home front, turning out replacement planes and tanks, and the ships in which to send them over, as well as K-rations, ammunition, and uniforms. And who was producing all of that? In large part, the women."

So this volume is a historical record of those times, written from each woman's experience, with details as she remembers them. But it is also a tribute to the phenomenal contributions that these women — and others like them — made to America, Americans, and the world. Their stories remind us that, though World War II is over, we still have a job to do. Freedom is still in need of protection. Loyalty and patriotism are still values to be employed against tyranny. The "We Can Do It!" spirit of the World War II Rosies must never die. Now and always, Americans can and must consciously decide that "We Can *Still* Do It!"

Rosies, your gift is still giving, and we accept it with grateful hearts!

Nell Carter Branum
ARRA Book Editor

CONTENTS

1. Women of World War II, *Stanley* 1

2. Secretary for the War Effort, *Leuck* 3

3. Making the Atomic Bomb in Oak Ridge, *Harper* 5

4. Growing Up, *Hrabec* 7

5. Who Remembers Rosie the Riveter? *Johnson/Croker* . 9

6. Boeing Aircraft Rosie, *Angell* 11

7. I Was Betty, the Solderer's Assistant., *Brooks* 13

8. Taking the First Steps for the War Effort, *Armstrong*. 15

9. Making Parachutes for the War Effort, *Lewis* 17

10. From School to Work for the War Effort., *Lewis* ... 19

11. Rat-a-Tat-Tat: Working on Navy Bombers, *Payant*. .21

12. Shipbuilders: Side by Side, *Woodruff* 23

13. Greetings from an Arizona Rosie, *Yanacek* 25

14. Engineering Design for the War Effort, *Domenick*. . 27

15. From Farm to Aircraft Factory, *Nakashima*. 29

16. Build a Ship to Bring Him Home, *Grant* 31

17. Wartime Changes, *Pearson* 33

18. Boeing's First Woman Riveter, *McMasters*. 35

19. Never Underestimate the Power of a 37
    Woman, *Brady*

20. Small Town Gal, Bomber Builder, *Jones* 39

21. How Are Your Splices?, *Mock* 41

22. Rosie the Riveter, *Lorette* 43

23. The War of a Century, *Rojas* 45

24. From Schoolteacher and Mother 47
    to Riveting Instructor, *Irvin*

25. My Call to Serve, *Fredricksen*. 49

26. Remarkable Roxie, *Turney* 51

27. The Battle of Seattle, *Ash* 53

28. My World War II Experiences, *Taylor*. 55

29. From Riveting to Driving, *Felton* 57

30. Change Order, *Nichols* 59

31. Rosie Jane Helps the War Effort, *Chason*. 61

32. From Hawaii, Dec. 7, to V-J Day, Chicago, *Nist* ... 63

33. They Called Me "Josie the Riveter," *Paddock* 65

34. My Days as Rosie the Riveter, *Ryan*............. 67

35. Our Wartime Heroine, *Burkhardt* 69

36. The Blind Riveter, *Sherrow*................... 71

37. A Centenarian Rosie, *Pringle*................. 73

38. B-29 a Reality, *Doebbeling*................... 75

39. Dorothy Goes To the City, *Martin*.............. 77

40. From Farm Field to Airfield, *Wilkins*...........79

41. The Early Years, *Stoutamire* 81

42. Eighteen, *Collier*............................83

43. My Contribution to the WW II Effort, *Tinker*...... 85

44. WW II Influence On My Lifetime Career, *Hamilton*. 87

45. Pistol Packin' Mama, *Barrett* 89

46. My Experience As a "Rosie," *Hill* 91

47. An Oklahoma Rosie, *Highsmith* 93

48. Just Married Four Months, *Jayme*.............. 95

49. My Experience As a Secretary in the 97
    Pentagon, WW II, *Myrick*

50. Marian the Machinist, *Fox*.................... 99

51. Rosie the Riveter, *Blume*.....................101

52. World War II: The Story of 103
    Nora Willis, *Willis*

53. Women at Work in Detroit Defense Plants, ... 105
    Zublin

54. My Parachute Story: A Packer and 107
    Government Inspector, *Putnam*

55. Steel for Warships, *Dalzell* 109

56. I Built Airplanes So the Boys Could. 111
    Win the War, *Norick*

57. Lela's "Rosie" Uniform, *McDaniel*. 113

58. True Love Still Exists, *Sedwick*. 115

59. The Family Rose Garden, *Van Betten*. 117

60. Rosie Times Two, *Beard* 119

61. Have Rivet Gun, Will Travel, *Berry* 121

62. My Story as Rosie the Riveter, *Shaffer*. 123

63. From Farm Girl to Factory Worker, *Du Lac*. 125

64. A Day In the Life of a Rosie the Riveter. 127
    During WW II, *Sargent*

65. High School and Wartime Memories, *Blackler* 129

66. Wanda the Welder, *Turner* 131

67. From Rosie to Retirement, *Fox*. 133

68. The Kansas Connection, *Salerno/Riley* 135

69. My First Job, *O'Quinn* 137

70. Lockheed Aircraft – That's Where I Was, ... 139
    Nikolaisen

71. Memories of "Rosie the Riveter" of WW II, ... 141
    Thomas

72. Rosie the Riveter, *Hasty* 143

73. We Fought the Home Front Battle, *Van Alstine* 145

74. My Rosie the Riveter Experience – WW II, *Logan*. 147

75. My Mom As a Rosie the Riveter, *Logan/Hoines* . . .149

76. I Was Working on the Railroad, *Kessler* 151

77. A Shipyard Worker and Volunteer Nurse, ...153
    Matheny

78. Gun-Smithing in World War II, *Fix* 155

79. The Gold B-17, *Stevenson/Philley* 157

80. I Loved Those Planes, *Hoaglund* 159

81. Auntie El, a Rosie the Riveter, *Fortner/Hanke* 161

82. The Wooden Leg, *Levitas* .163

83. World War II Memories, *Anderson* 165

84. My Work for the War Effort, *Johnson* 167

85. Perhaps the Youngest B-29 Riveter, *Lund* 169

86. My "Rosie" Story, *Zimmerman* 171

87. A World War II Romance, *Sellers* 173

88. Want To Do More, *Posko* 175

89. My Years As a Rosie, *Donohue* 177

90. Rosie the Riveter, *Smith* 179

91. Happy Times at Boeing, *Bumgardner*. 181

92. Shipyard Welder, *Lane* 183

93. The Good Old Days, *Hamilton* 185

94. Ole Rosie of World War II, *Carter* 187

95. Two Years I'll Never Forget, *Clayberger*. 189

96. The Story of a Rosie, *Belcher/Young*. 191

97. A Real Pistol Packin' Mamma, *Field*   193

98. Rosie the Riveter, *Morrissette*. 195

99. My Assemblyline Extended Family, *Aulger*. 197

100. Teletypist Rosie, *Updike*. 199

101. The Rosie Story of Susan T. King, *King* 201

102. Liberator Bombers, *Tretheway* 203

103. A Family Full of Rosies, *Pazdro* 205

104. My Work for the Railroad, *Booth* 207

Index 209

American Rosie the Riveter Association® 213

Books Published by ARRA® 214

WOMEN OF WORLD WAR II

by Lessie Hendon Stanley
Whitesburg, Georgia

Lessie Mae Hendon Stanley in 1941 and in 2002

My name is Lessie Hendon Stanley. When the U. S. was attacked by Japan, I was not quite 17 years old, and I guess I did not realize the horror of war. In 1942, after I turned 17, I was dating a boy from our church who had turned 19. His name was George Stanley. We talked about getting married then, as we knew he would have to go into the service. He joined the Navy, and we decided to wait until he came home after the war to get married. He was gone until February 21, 1945. We were married March 1, 1945.

Soon after the war started, Firestone took over the Lakewood Chevrolet plant, and turned it into a plant to make floats and wings for the planes called "Black Cats," which were mostly patrol planes. My sister and I lived only a few miles from the plant, so we both got jobs there at the same time. Her name was Jean Hendon Hammond. She was married with one small boy. We were lucky to be partners on the float line driving rivets. She was 5'7" tall and I was 5'4" tall. Since she was the tallest and could reach over the floats better, she did the bucking and I did the riveting. It was not real hard work, but was strenuous at times.

We could not do sloppy work. The rivets could not be dented or creased. We had to use cold rivets. If we let them get to room temperature, they would not drive. If a rivet was dented or cut, we had to drill it out and most of the time, we had to drill a larger hole and use a larger rivet, which didn't make the boss happy.

We didn't have many accidents on the front line, but they had a bad one on the wing line. A girl with real long hair got it caught in a rod turning down the middle of the wing. The poor girl died later. This taught us all a lesson.

My only accident was with my foreman. One day, I was taping inside the float and about all you could see of me was my legs and feet. He came up and stuck his head in to see how I was doing. I turned to see who it was. I was wearing red lipstick and when I turned, I got red lipstick all over his white shirt. His wife was not happy about this. I was riding to work with him then, and she made him stop picking me up. I really was sorry about it, but she would never believe what happened. She never liked me after that.

George came home in February of 1945 and we were married. I went to the plant where I worked to let them know that I was quitting. They said that I couldn't quit because I worked for the government. But I told them that I was going to Boston with my husband and that they would have to come and get me. OK, they didn't. By then, I realized how terrible the war was, as I was losing so many friends and schoolmates, and so many came back crippled in some way, either physically or mentally.

SECRETARY FOR THE WAR EFFORT
by Eleanor "Mickie" Clyden Leuck
Sun City West, Arizona

Eleanor "Mickie" Clyden Leuck

I was a senior in high school when war was declared. What a frightening day it was when we were all called to the meeting room and we listened to the President give his speech. Several of my male classmates immediately signed up for the service.

Being the middle one of eleven children, it was necessary for me to earn my own money to attend secretarial school, which was my goal. I took the test and was selected to go to Washington, D. C. as a Grade I Secretary, but my parents objected so strongly, I didn't go. I have often wondered how different my life would have been, had I gone.

After graduation, I went to work at Food Machinery

Corporation, which was now a war production plant. Wallace Walsh was made War Production Manager, and I became his secretary. It was a challenging, enjoyable position. I was issued a typewriter with an extra-long carriage, and I prepared and typed all war forms, with page after page of numbers that were highly confidential.

I completed secretarial college at night, along with rolling Red Cross bandages. We went weekly on a supervised bus to Chanute Field Air Force Base to dance with the service men.

Everyone in our town of Hoopeston, Illinois pitched in to help the war effort and did whatever was needed. Remember the ration books that soon followed? They were used to purchase gas, tires, shoes, sugar, etc. I still have mine, minus some stamps. Nylons, film, and many other things we took for granted were not available. We put makeup on our legs instead of nylons.

The "younger generation" would never believe the sacrifices everyone made, but we did it before, and we would do it again. God Bless America!

MAKING THE ATOMIC BOMB IN OAK RIDGE, TENNESSEE
by Hazel Owenby Harper
Mineral Bluff, Georgia

Hazel Harper in the 1940's (left) and more recently

In 1942, in the hills of Tennessee, with plenty of water, a railroad nearby, and roads for cars and trucks, the city of Oak Ridge was built almost overnight. It was called "The City Behind the Fence" because it was a city that was completely fenced. It had approximately seven gates to enter and exit through, and these gates were guarded by civilian and Army police.

Three plants were inside the fenced city, and each plant was fenced in, also. The three plants were named Y-12, K-25, and X-10. We had churches, schools, stores, movie theaters, and a skating rink. The stores were open 24 hours a day, 7 days a week, 12 months a year. We had many things that were not available in other stores because of rationing. The drugstores had snack bars, and this was a great place to hang out with friends. Sometimes we would ride the bus to the end of the line and back, just for the fun of it. This didn't always make the driver happy.

At age 23, I moved to Oak Ridge, along with my sister, Gladys Owenby. We rented a room in a private home, and we both began working.

I worked in the Y-12 plant during 1944-45. My job was to operate a series of meters that were located in four separate cubicles. Each metal cubicle was approximately six feet wide and ten feet high, and contained 10-15 meters. The meter readings had to be kept balanced, with the Q's up and the R's down. The plant operated on 8-hour shifts, 24 hours a day.

We were only allowed into our specific work area. Guards were everywhere, and you'd better have your badge! When we took a restroom break, we had to make sure a co-worker was operating our meters in addition to the me-

Oak Ridge, Tennessee in 1943

ters she operated. Everything was clothed in secrecy! We knew we were working on something important, and possibly dangerous, pertaining to the war, but we had no idea what. After the Atomic Bomb was dropped on Hiroshima, Japan in 1945, we knew! The first cubicle was shut down. Co-workers referred to it as having died, and a huge wreath of flowers was hung on the wall of meters. We were grateful to God that we would have peace again!

GROWING UP
by Joyce D. "Zack" Hrabec
Sun City West, Arizona

Joyce D. "Zack" Hrabec

In our last semester of school, the boys decided to join the cooking class. A few of us girls decided to take drafting. Prior to graduation, our school counselor told us that the Signal Corps was offering a class at Washburn High School to teach us various techniques of mechanical tools and their uses, so I signed up for the course on Saturdays. At the end of the course, I was given a diploma and a form to fill out for the possibility of a job in California or Washington state.

The opportunity to travel really sounded wonderful. So I happily brought the paperwork home – and everything came to a dead halt. No, I could not accept the offer!! I was underage. My mother, my two brothers, and my sister vetoed my dreams, and Mother would not sign. What a disappointment!

So I volunteered to work at the USO downtown in Chicago on Friday nights. My Economics teacher, a World War I veteran who had been injured in battle and had a silver plate in his head, would give me a carton of cigarettes to take to the canteen. Our cafeteria would furnish a cake. So off I would go to do my duty at the USO. Seeing the boys come in, especially those who just arrived after being in combat, and seeing their beat-up uniforms, made me realize just what war was about.

After graduation in June, 1943, I applied for work at Danly Machine Specialties in Cicero, Illinois, and was hired as a Precision Inspector. My training had paid off. I would inspect all kinds of parts, checking to make certain that they were manufactured to precise tolerances as required on the blueprints. They would be the foundation for the gun carriages that would be placed upon them on the ships.

As the war finally wound down, I realized that hopefully my endeavors to support our troops had somehow helped. They also taught me the pleasures of volunteering, which I support to this day.

WHO REMEMBERS ROSIE THE RIVETER?

by Ann Johnson of Lompoc, California
As told to her daughter, Joyce Croker

Ann Ramirez Johnson in 1940 and now

Who remembers Rosie the Riveter? I do, because I was one of many women who worked in the shipyard in 1942. Before the shipyards, at the age of 24, I worked as a beautician in a beauty shop in Oakland, California for $17 a week. One of the other beauty operators, Lucille DeAndre, started working the midnight shift at the shipyards, making $50 a week, and she said it was fun. The next day I applied for work. Lucille was the first burner, and I was the second in Yard Three, working for Kaiser shipyards in Point Richmond, California.

Our boss, Chick DeAndre, first instructed us in the art of the hand burner. We had to learn how to keep the tip of the acetylene clean so we could combine the acetylene with oxygen to obtain the right amount of pressure for the hand burner to make a smooth, clean cut through different kinds of steel. We also had to learn which needles to use on various thicknesses of steel. In the plate shop, we learned how to use the travel graft. This involved using two or three torches at one time to cut several sheets of steel for the ships. After a couple of weeks, we became instructors for new people coming in.

I remember that we used to have fun at lunchtime. We enjoyed making new friends, and some guys wanted to date us. However, we did not want to. So they got even with us by putting red paint on our bench. We sat down, unaware of the prank played on us. When we got up, everyone was laughing at us and we didn't understand why. We had red paint on our pants!

Jewel Newell and I got even by making some chocolate candy and putting three boxes of Ex-Lax in it to give to all the fellows. The day after we gave out the candy, the guys who came to work were sick, and some did not even show up for work. We felt good that we got back at them, but we felt very unpatriotic that they missed work. Everyone had a good laugh afterward, and we all remained friends.

World War II brought many losses for everyone. My first boyfriend, Antonio Velansques, died in the war, which gave me a great appreciation for our veterans and the sacrifices they made for our country.

One good thing came out of the war. I met my husband, Warren Johnson, who was a shrinker in the shipyards. He wanted me to give him a permanent to live up to his nickname, Curly. This changed my name from Andrea Ramirez to Ann Johnson. I am fortunate to have three children and five grandchildren.

BOEING AIRCRAFT ROSIE
by Jan Angell
Pahrump, Nevada

No photo available

I was working as a drive-in waitress in 1941 when we all heard the radio announcement that we were at war with the Japanese. I was really sorry to hear this, but I didn't know the reason why or what would come up later in life. I was working in Renton, Washington. This area was completely surrounded by Japanese farmers. The farms were as nice as I have ever seen.

The radio and newspapers were crying for defense workers. My folks and I moved to Seattle, where I was hired as a riveter in Boeing Aircraft. I was trying to learn to be a riveter when no one seemed to know. I would have hated to ride in the first plane that was put out, but I guess we must have done a fairly good job, since it flew.

It was not a good place to be a bucker. We were on opposite sides and the bucker had to lie on the floor while the riveter did her job. Of course, if it was hot and you were on the floor, smelling the feet was not so good! Luckily, I learned quickly and was on the other side. I made sure that my feet were clean.

We had quite a few sirens for air raids. We had to drop everything and get out of the building. Our building had a lot of camouflage, but we weren't far from the coast.

A person living in Seattle lived on hills. I had a Model-T Ford, and every time I took it out I had to change a tire since tires were so scarce. You had to take care of what you had. My Ford didn't have much in the way of brakes, so when I was coming down the hill I would have to turn off the motor, and the car would come to a halt.

I really enjoyed my job, but later quit my job in Seattle and moved to Portland, where I became a welder. You learn a lot from people when you're all in the same boat and have to give up some things that you're used to having.

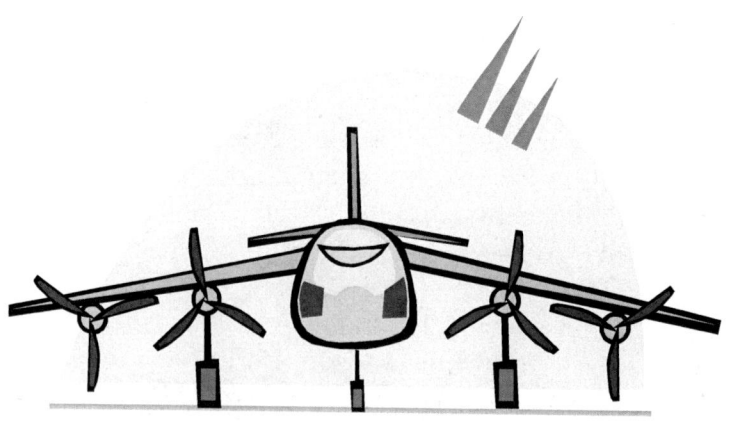

I WAS BETTY, THE SOLDERER'S ASSISTANT
by Elizabeth Betterley Brooks
Bradenton, Florida

Left: Claude and Elizabeth (Betty) Brooks at Boise, Idaho, Claude's last assignment before he left for Italy. He completed 35 missions as a ball gunner in B-24's. Right: Elizabeth in 2004 at the age of 87.

"So this is Precision Parts," I thought, as I approached the warehouse-like building that I had come to Dexter, Michigan to see. I had seen my husband, Claude, off for overseas duty, and had promised to stay overnight with friends from Maine who were living in Ann Arbor.

These good friends knew that, without Claude, I didn't have much reason to go back to Maine. I could teach school in Ann Arbor as well as in Maine, and the pay would be much better. Both the Army and the Air Force had refused me for being too short and too light in weight. My friends said, "This is the place to be."

A glance at the want ads told me there were thousands wanted for factory jobs. Well, I got a job, all right. They started me doing something with a screwdriver, and at the end of a long and painful day, I had more band-aids than finished parts. I was sure they would fire me.

They didn't. They bumped me up to a solderer's section and gave me a wonderful partner. She warmed to me and I warmed to her. Although I was supposed to be her assistant, she did her work and helped me when I fell behind in mine.

I must have been a curious sight. I wore Maine casual wear, which consisted of wool slacks, a lumber-man's flannel shirt, and ski boots. Many of the women came to work in high heels, nylons, and silk dresses. My accent was so strongly Maine that some people thought I was English. I was different. There were others who were different, too.

Slowly I got to know everyone in the factory. There were very few men, and many of them were retired. But 90 per cent were women, of all ages and all walks of life.

I soon became a curiosity because I kept my private life private. They only knew that I was there because my husband was flying out of Italy in B-24 bombers – and we were a factory making precision parts for B-24's. Soon I was treated like a minor celebrity, my clothes and accent and reticence setting me apart.

They really respected me. I didn't really realize this until I was about to leave and, to my great surprise, they held a potluck dinner right in the middle of the factory for me, with the owner and big shots, as well as the workers. As a going-away gift, I was presented with a sterling silver candy dish, as well as congratulations that I had stuck it out until my husband had returned, having finished his missions. They had never had a going-away party before. As I polish that candy dish today, I always think how good it is to remember the days when most everyone had the same motive: "Let's get this war won!"

TAKING THE FIRST STEPS FOR THE WAR EFFORT

by Helen M. Ensey Armstrong
El Mirage, Arizona

Helen Ensey Armstrong (right) and her sister, Audrey Ensey Mikulsky, in Seattle in 1942

In 1942, it was lonesome in our little farming town of Morgan, Minnesota. All of the boys and our closest girlfriends had gone off to join the war. What were a young gal and her sister to do? My fun-loving, outgoing sister, Audrey, had an idea. She wanted to get one of those good-paying factory jobs that we had been reading and hearing about. We thought that way we'd make some good money and find a little more fun. We decided to talk to our parents about it. They always gave us good advice and then supported our decisions. They said they'd be sorry to see us go, but thought it was a good idea.

My dad drove us to the War Training Center in Wilmar, Minnesota, and wished us well. Even though we were only about 50 miles from home, it seemed so far away and we were a bit scared to be in this new town alone. We stayed in a dormitory with eight or ten other girls. Audrey and I quickly made friends with the other girls. All of us gals were in the same boat – away from home for the first time at the start of an uncertain adventure. We all pitched in to help each other out.

Even in this large town, the only men around were our teachers. My first project was making a little coal shuttle, which taught me blueprint-reading, metal-cutting, welding, drilling, and riveting. It wasn't too daunting, as I had done similar things on the farm. Our classroom days were over in a few weeks, and then we were given our choice of factories in several cities. We decided on the Boeing plant in Seattle because our father's sister, Hallie, lived in Spokane and could help us if we needed it. The War Training Center gave us train fare to Seattle and away we went once again, just my sister and I.

It was winter and the scenery was white with snow. It was exciting to see so much of our beautiful country. The train was bursting with life as we headed to a destination where we had no idea what to expect. Seattle looked huge to us farm girls. The streets seemed to be filled with flowers. We lived in a boarding house that Boeing had arranged and paid for until we could find our own accommodations in a week or so. Our little rooms were clean, friendly, and within walking distance of the factory. No one had cars in those days and there was gas rationing.

Audrey and I enjoyed it all after we adjusted to the big city, factory life, and (the easiest part) dancing with the boys. Our big adventure, scary as it started out, turned out fine as I drilled rivet holes on the fuselage of first B-17 bombers, and then the huge B-29's. We both stayed happily married to the men we met in Seattle.

MAKING PARACHUTES FOR THE WAR EFFORT
by Dorothy "Lucy" Case Lewis
Birmingham, Alabama

Lucy Lewis at age 18 while her husband, Robert, was overseas (left), and with Robert in 2001

When WW II started in 1941, I was in high school in Birmingham, Alabama. I was 15 years old, and I remember listening to President Roosevelt on the radio, saying that Japan had bombed Pearl Harbor, and that we were at war. I was not afraid of being bombed, but I was sad because I knew so many of my friends would have to fight in the war.

I had been dating a boy that I went to school with, Robert Lewis, who was out of school and working at U. S. Steel. He was 19 and when I was 16, we were married in Leesville, Louisiana. My sister's boyfriend was stationed there and we had a double wedding in a Baptist church.

Soon after we were married, Robert was drafted, and

after 13 weeks he was sent to north Africa with the 9th Infantry Division. He was gone for three years, and never had a leave until October, 1945.

After Robert was drafted, I heard about a plant that was making parachutes, the Dixie Manufacturing Company. I applied for a job and was hired. I had to get a permit to work because I was so young. I worked on a commercial sewing machine, sewing seams and tabs for the ropes to go through. There were no air conditioners or restaurants, so we took our lunch every day. Most of the workers were young girls, with a few men in management or maintenance. It was hard work, but it was fun working with all the girls. We made $.50 an hour and worked 10 hours a day, 5 days a week.

There were very few cars and you couldn't buy gasoline, so everyone rode streetcars to work, which took quite a while. But they ran regularly, about every 5 or 10 minutes.

There was not much going on for entertainment. Sometimes there were parties and there was dancing at a local park. And there was the USO.

Robert was wounded in the invasion of Normandy and received the Purple Heart. He also received a Distinguished Unit Badge with one Oak Leaf Cluster, a Good Conduct Medal, European, African, and Middle Eastern Service Medals, one Silver Star and one Bronze Star.

After the war ended, the plant closed where I worked. I didn't work again until our son decided to go to medical school. I worked at University of Alabama at Birmingham for 10 years, and at Rust Engineering Company until 1983.

My son, Dr. Jerry K. Lewis, was in Family Practice Medicine for 30 years in Birmingham until September, 2003, when he died of cancer. My husband also had cancer and passed away in June, 2001. I miss them so much.

I am proud of my work for the war effort and Robert's time in the service. I am thankful he came home and that we had 59 wonderful years together. I am proud to be a Rosie and to live in America.

FROM SCHOOL TO WORK FOR THE WAR EFFORT

by Dorothy Lewis
Sister of Nell Case Morgan Lewis
Midfield, Alabama

Nell Case Lewis in the 1940's

I am writing this in memory of my sister, Nell, who passed away in September, 1984. We were a family of seven children, living on a large farm in Tennessee, when our father died in 1931. Nell was nine years old at the time, and I was five. We moved to Birmingham to be close to my mother's family.

We attended the schools there. At the time WW II started, we were in high school. Nell was a beautiful girl, and very popular. In our family, the three youngest girls were the only ones left at home then. All the others were married with families or in the service. Nell was always referred to as the pretty one, which was true.

When Nell was out of high school, she worked at a family-owned grocery store on the corner from where we lived, until Bechtel McCombs Parsons Aircraft opened their plant at the Birmingham airport. She applied for a job there and was hired to work in the Blueprint Department. Our brother, who was a good bit older and had a family, worked there, too. He worked as an electrician.

Nell was dating a sailor who was in the Pacific, Oswald Morgan, and they were married when he came home from the war.

We always had good times together, we three girls. Everything was rationed and there were very few cars, so we all rode streetcars to work. We didn't have much money, but a lot of fun. Once, Nell didn't have money to go to the movies when we were still in school. There was a talent show that if you entered, you could see the movie. She entered and sang "Have You Ever Been Lonely" and was admitted. I will always remember that, because she had never sung in public before – and, I think, never did again. We also went to parties and got together with friends.

After the war ended and the plant closed at the airport, Nell stayed home with her family, two boys and a girl. She was proud of her work for the war effort. She passed away of a heart attack in 1984.

Nell and her sister, Dorothy Lewis, in 1943

RAT-A-TAT-TAT: WORKING ON NAVY BOMBERS

by Elizabeth A. "Liz" Payant
Sun City West, Arizona

Elizabeth Ann Lee, age 19, in her Cadet Nurse Corps uniform, University of Michigan School of Nursing, 1944.

After graduating from Kingsford High School in Michigan's Upper Peninsula in 1943, I went to Detroit to find work to help with college expenses. I had been accepted into the University of Michigan's School of Nursing. I got a job at Hudson Motor Car Company and enrolled in riveting school. My partner who "bucked" for me was a classy lady named Helen from Grosse Pointe, Michigan. Her husband was a Lieutenant in the Air Force.

Helen and I won all the riveting contests, but after six weeks, Hudson had to release us because there was no place for us in their plant. So off we went to Chrysler Motor across the street. Since we had learned our trade well, they put us in Final Assembly with the Navy inspectors. It was a great job walking around with them, changing rivets whenever they found a faulty one.

I had been warned about our foreman, Scotty. He was a mean sun-of-a-gun, they said, so I should keep a low profile. One day I was waiting for the inspectors. A nice, gray-haired fellow was standing beside me.

"Do you know Scotty?" I asked.

"Yeah."

"Well, when you see him, will you please point him out to me? I hear he's a bear, and I don't want to get in his way because I'm not going to be here very long."

"Yeah?"

"Well, I'm gong to nursing school and will be a Cadet Nurse in February, and I'm working just until then, so if you see him, let me know. Is he around now?"

"Yeah – I'm Scotty," was the terse answer.

Well, that nice gray-haired man took very good care of me, shooing would-be suitors away, and taking me aside once in awhile to see how things were going financially. No one could understand why Scotty was so nice to me, the new kid on the block. On my last day, he told me he had a daughter in nursing school.

There were 76 in my freshman class. Twenty-six graduated. Eight-hour shifts that never ended in eight hours took their toll, along with tough classes with tougher instructors. We did the bulk of the work in the hospital since most of the RN's were in service. We were never obligated to the government for our Cadet Nurse schooling, but we were forever grateful for our education.

I have met many nurses over the years, but never a riveter until recently. A cousin whom we were visiting in Wyoming had another house guest, who had also been a riveter. We decided to play "20 Questions" with the others. We asked, "What do we have in common other than we are from Michigan and female?" On the fourteenth question, my husband Bill shouted, "Riveters!"

SHIPBUILDERS: SIDE BY SIDE

by Easter Reynolds Jones Woodruff
Montgomery, Alabama

Easter Jones (in center with white scarf), a welder from 1943-1945, with fellow shipbuilders

During WW II, from 1943 to 1945, my first husband, Joe Jones, and I worked as welders for McCloskey's Shipbuilding company at Hooker's Point in Tampa, Florida. The company had sent both of us to welding classes at a local vocational school after the demand for wartime vessels steadily increased with the escalation of the war. I doubled up on my classes because I wanted to be an expert welder, and I knew it would be hard competing with men in this field.

Joe and I were involved in the production of cargo ships that were sent to overseas ports where our allies used them as underwater barriers. These sunken vessels prevented the Japanese from invading many harbors in the Pacific territories.

My job was to weld the temporary bulkhead into place until the permanent walls were installed. One day, a bulkhead collapsed in a ship in the basin next to mine, killing three men. The leaderman reported that the accident was caused from careless welding. He wouldn't let me, a woman, view the gruesome scene. I was thankful I wasn't one of the welders responsible for the tragedy.

Company officials wouldn't allow a husband and wife to work on the same ship – too much personal and professional competition! Once the leaderman brought Joe over to my ship to show him the great welding job I had performed on a poop deck. I was so proud of my accomplishment! Joe just quietly nodded in agreement.

Joe and I each earned $93 a week; we saved one check and lived on the other. We lived in shipyard apartments and paid $32 a month, utilities included. We paid $3.25 a week for our youngest son, Faires, to stay at the shipyard nursery. Neighbors kept our other son, Franky, for $10 a week. We were fortunate to have so much money after enduring many hardships during the Depression.

Easter with Joe, who passed away in 1975

Joe had purchased some new tires for our car. On the last day of the war, when we were leaving the shipyard after work, we discovered that our car had been jacked up and out brand new tires had been stolen! Joe had to go to the other side of Tampa and buy some used tires. When he returned in a borrowed car, I had to drive our car, without my license and with our two baby sons, back across town!

I will always remember the crowds of people dancing in the streets of Tampa after the war was over, celebrating the end of an emotional four years. I just wanted to go home – so happy that Joe and I had played a crucial role in defeating the Japanese.

GREETINGS FROM AN ARIZONA ROSIE

by Mescal P. Yanacek
Salem, Oregon

Mescal Yanacek in the 1940's

Some friends and I were enjoying a holiday in the mountains above Roosevelt Lake when we heard the announcement over the car radio that war had been declared. I can still hear the sadness in the President's voice when he said that Pearl Harbor had been attacked by the Japanese. We returned to Phoenix as quickly as possible. We were deeply affected and, truthfully, frightened, having no idea what the future would bring.

Arizona adjusted quickly, and soon there was a call for volunteers. Women were needed for work at Goodyear, as well as at the canteen and USO. I made and served many, many cakes and hundreds of cups of coffee.

I was working as a Licensed Practical Nurse at the time, but could not resist the call for women at Goodyear. I started working on floats that would help a plane stay afloat if it landed in water. From there I went to the Blueprint Department, from which I asked to be transferred. I began working in the Drilling section. The drills ranged from about 1½ inches to about 10 inches. This was delicate, precise work, and caution was your warning.

A call came for a rivet team to work on the High Jigs. This job needed both strength and a steady hand. I had both, so my partner, Anna Ash, and I worked on the High Jigs until the plant closed. She was the riveter and I was the bucker. We worked with both the usual rivets and the Ice Box rivets. Anna and I lost touch through the years, so Anna, if you are reading this, please contact me.

The one frustrating thing that I remember was a joker who would slip up behind a worker and shove an imitation snake in your face. I think he finally got canned, for this prank was offensive and dangerous.

I met an awful lot of nice people at Goodyear, and I still treasure the memories.

Mescal Yanacek in 2003

ENGINEERING DESIGN FOR THE WAR EFFORT

by Mary Lou FitzGerald Domenick
Jeannette, Pennsylvania

Mary Lou Domenick in 1943 (left) and in 2004

It was June, 1943. I was 17 years old and I was graduating from Jeannette High School. The night of the graduation exercise, I realized how many of the boys in our class were leaving within the next week to join the military service. I knew what they were going to do, but I did not know what the future held for me.

I had thoughts about going to college to study theater arts at Carnegie Tech in Pittsburgh, Pennsylvania. Theater arts – music, drama, and writing – held a great interest for me. I was waiting for my family to give the "OK" when fate stepped in.

A neighbor of mine worked in the office of Hockensmith Company in Penn, Pennsylvania. This company had three divisions: Hockensmith Wheel & Mine Car Company,

Superior Mold & Iron Company, and Penn Body. I was told they were looking for a girl to do engineering drawing as a draftsman. All of their draftsmen except for one older man had been called to the service.

I went for the interview and was hired. I agreed to attend classes five evenings per week from 6:00 to 9:00 p.m. at Penn State Extension in Greensburg, a part of Penn State University. Within two months, I was drawing for Superior Mold in Ingot Mold Design. Ingot molds are used to hold molten iron when it is poured by a giant ladle from the furnace. It is a very important part of steel production.

I did drawings for steel plants in Pennsylvania, Ohio, Indiana, Illinois, Maryland, Michigan, and West Virginia. A pencil drawing was made of the ingot mold according to the specifications needed by the steel company. Then I made an ink tracing on special tracing paper of the pencil design, and a blueprint was made from this tracing.

When I would take my blueprints to the Pattern Shop, all of the men in the factory would stop working and watch me walk by, as I was the first woman ever hired by this company.

I worked for Superior Mold & Iron Company from June, 1943 to September, 1945 when the war was won.

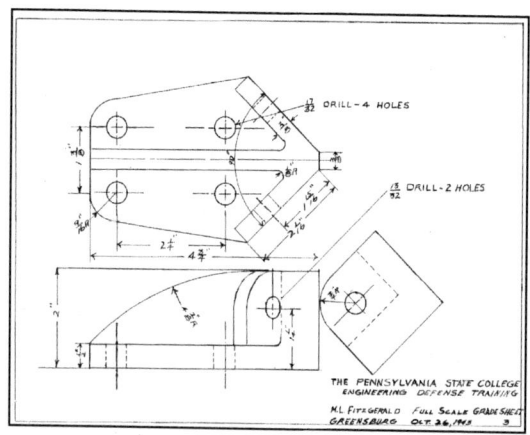

One of Mary Lou's drawings from 1943

FROM FARM TO AIRCRAFT FACTORY

by
Signe E. "Sig" Olson Nakashima

Ridgecrest, California

Signe E. Olson Gallaher in 1942, two months before moving to California

In November, 1942, my late husband and I moved from Nebraska to California to get into "war work." We hired into Lockheed Aircraft Corporation in Burbank, California the next month and received the *big* wages – 66 cents an hour! We worked on the swing shift, 4:30 p.m. to 1:00 a.m., six days a week, receiving time-and-a-half for overtime. Coming from the farm where $1.00 a day was the going rate, we thought we were rich.

My title was "riveter." I worked on several aircraft parts, including PV-2 air scoops, P-38 fuselages, and B-17 cowlings. Because ladies usually had long hair, we were required to wear caps known as "snoods." They were not flattering, but we got used to them and they probably saved us from some serious injuries.

Since I had grown up on a farm and was familiar with tools, I was also given the job of training other ladies in the use of hand tools. Some of the ladies had never held a hand tool. One lady even tried to use a pair of pliers with both hands. I think the hack saw was their biggest challenge.

After a couple of years, they transferred me to the Rework Section, where we received damaged airplane parts. We were required to determine if the parts should be repaired or scrapped and if repairable, to fix them. I was transferred there as an experiment – to see if a woman was capable of doing this kind of work. I worked out fine; in fact, I loved the work. What they didn't realize at the time was that, given the chance, a woman could do anything a man could, provided it was within her physical capabilities.

At the end of the war, we moved to the China Lake Navy Base on the Mojave Desert in California, where we pursued work with the federal government. I eventually became an Electronic Technician, where I was able to take advantage of some of my mechanical experience from Lockheed. I retired in 1976.

*Signe Esther Nakashima
in 2004*

BUILD A SHIP
TO BRING HIM HOME
by Kate Grant
Moore, Oklahoma

Melvin, Kate, and Laquetta Grant in the 1940's

In 1943, I became a welder in the Richmond Shipyards in California. I worked the graveyard shift from midnight to 8:00 a.m. I had leather gloves and pants, a big hood, goggles, and a leather jacket. I held the welding rod in one hand and the torch fire in the other. I placed the rod in a seam and melted it down in a small bead and brushed it off with a steel brush. During the war, that yard built and sent 747 ships and 60,000 tanks into battle. One time, we built a Liberty Ship, start to finish, in an astounding four and a half days.

My husband, Melvin, shipped out on September 11, 1944. My 16-month-old daughter, Laquetta, and I moved into a rented three-bedroom house in Pittsburgh, California.

My sister, Idell, and her three sons moved in with us when her husband, Potter, shipped out in October. We split the duties of child-rearing while working separate shifts. I worked at the John Mansville Roofing Company from 8:00 a.m. to 4:00 p.m., and Idell worked at the fountain, serving sandwiches and sodas from 5:00 to 11:00 p.m. Idell took care of the kids during the day, and when I got home she would have the washing done, the kids fed, and dinner ready for me. I would put the kids to bed, do all the ironing, and clean the house. Then I would write a letter to Melvin and cry. On Sundays, Laquetta and I would go to the park.

One day in July, Idell received a telegram stating that Potter had been killed. Idell, in her grief, lost touch with the world for a month. Later, Mama asked her, "What happened to you?" Idell replied, "Potter came to me in a dream and told me to get up and raise these boys."

When Melvin came home from the war in the Pacific in 1945, like most women war workers, I returned to the home. I never forgot my experiences or the thrill of getting a chance to do my part for the war effort.

Kate and Melvin Grant

WARTIME CHANGES
by Eleanor L. Pearson
Vancouver, Washington

Eleanor Pearson, welder, at age 18 in 1943 (left), and in front of an LST at Higgins Shipyard in 1944

I turned 16 a little over a week after President Roosevelt announced that we were at war. In 1942, I dropped out of school and joined millions of women taking wartime jobs that were held previously by men.

I applied for work at the Kaiser Shipyard in Vancouver, Washington, and was hired as a scaler. This was a miserable job, which involved crawling around in the double bottoms of ships on the ways. I came home every night, covered with rust.

I soon found there were welding classes available so I signed up, and in a short time I became proficient enough to work as a welder in the electric shop. I've always thought women make good welders because it's like sewing, using the welding rod as your needle and molten steel as the thread.

At the Vancouver yard, Liberty Ships and aircraft carriers were slipping down the ways in record time. I don't recall the number of employees, but I still remember my badge number, which was 41,859.

A special memory from this time was on April 5, 1943, when I joined a huge crowd of workers and visitors to witness Eleanor Roosevelt christening the aircraft carrier, U. S. S. Alazon Bay.

In the fall of 1943, I went to New Orleans, Louisiana, to stay with a relative, and had no problem hiring on at Higgins Industries Shipyard as a welder. General Dwight D. Eisenhower gave Andrew Higgins credit for winning the war with his revolutionary design that made amphibious landings possible, and said that without Higgins' boats, the whole strategy of the war would have been different.

In January of 1944, I was again home in Washington. I went to the recruiting office, thinking that now I was 18, that I could join the WAC's or the WAVE's, but learned I had to be 21. My age didn't prevent me from taking a civil service job as a civilian driver for the Army, at Vancouver Barracks.

The Barracks was a housing and embarkation point for troops coming and going overseas. It was also a holding point for a number of Italian prisoners of war. There were perhaps a dozen of us girls who worked out of the motor pool, driving trucks or staff cars. We girls did everything from shuttling men to and from the port to carrying a truckload of bread from the post bakery to the mess hall or chauffeuring officers. Sometimes we had a crew of POW's, and a guard with a shotgun on the back of our truck out on garbage detail.

When this job was phased out, I returned to Kaiser Shipyard as a welder, where I remained for the duration.

BOEING'S FIRST WOMAN RIVETER

by
Margot Bersos McMasters

Maple Valley, Washington

Margot McMasters, age 22, in 1942

I answered an ad for Seattle Boeing's first women's training school in May, 1942. I turned 22 that month. We were rushed to Boeing after a few days. Could I do what the men expected of me? I was sure going to try.

I worked as a rivet bucker on swing shift. We went to Plant 2 Final Assembly, and I was assigned to work on the bomb bay section of the B-17, from where they dropped bombs. There were absolutely no women when we came through, and I guess it looked pretty strange for the men working.

My supervisor, Ted Disch, told me to work with Owen McMasters. He would teach me how to buck rivets. It was exciting, knowing we were helping to win the war.

The men working with us were very good to us. Owen said I was great. We worked together for a few months.

Then on November 27, 1942, our foreman, Mr. Cliff, and our superintendent, Mr. Roberts, came over and told me they were upgrading me to riveter, and told me I was Boeing's first woman riveter. They arranged for MGM's Hollywood news team to come and take pictures of me, with my rivet bucker, riveting the top of the bomb bay section.

They always put MGM's roaring lion news highlights at the beginning of all movies that you went to see in those days. Several of us went to the movies to watch us on the news, and there we were, riveting on the top of the bomb bay section.

Later, I was also to be a pick-up riveter. My rivet bucker and I went into the finished planes before they went outside and repaired all of the damaged rivets.

Owen and I fell in love and were married in October, 1942. We have four children. He was drafted into the Army in 1945. He passed away in 1975 at age 55. Two of our sons now work at Boeing.

Margot McMasters

NEVER UNDERESTIMATE THE POWER OF A WOMAN
by Virginia Ellis Brady
Oklahoma City, Oklahoma

Virginia Ellis Brady with her sister, Iva Jean Ellis Easley, in their work uniforms in the 1940's (left), and with her husband, Howard, in 1998.

It was wartime for Virginia Ellis Brady and her sister, Iva Jean Ellis Easley, who were from a small town in southeastern Oklahoma called Wilburton. I (Virginia) had completed one year at Eastern A & M College. Jean had just completed high school.

For Jean, me, and other American women, the call to fill millions of jobs in factories, aircraft companies, and shipyards offered more than a steady paycheck. It represented a powerful act of patriotism and a chance for empowerment outside the kitchen. In my heart I felt as if I was really doing something for my country and the war effort.

Jean and I grabbed the chance for employment and never looked back. We had heard about good jobs at the

McDonnell Douglas Aircraft Plant in Oklahoma City. We packed our bags and caught a bus to Oklahoma City to live with our Aunt Mary and Uncle Earl.

For two years, I worked almost 50 hours a week as an engine rigger, installing the control rods on the C-47 engines of cargo planes. The control rods controlled the carburetor, throttle, start, etc. I learned to do many jobs inside the plane, like installing map tables, and other jobs using small tools such as the electric drill, jigsaw, copensaw, screwdrivers, and pliers. My sister, Jean, made cowlings (covers on the C-47 engines). She riveted the metal together. She married Lt. Mitchell B. Easley, who was a P-38 pilot.

As a security measure, each day as we entered the gates of the defense plant for work, we had to pass an entry examination, show our photo ID badge, and open our lunch boxes. We rode the city buses and carpooled to work, which was a distance of ten miles, one way.

On occasion, I needed to stop after work for business in the city. One evening, I was waiting for a green light to cross the street. Several soldiers drove by and flirted, and to my surprise they called me by my name, Virginia. I smiled when I realized that my name was on my lunch box.

During the war, certain items were rationed, such as gasoline, sugar, meat, shoes, tires, nylon hose, and other items that were important for the war effort. America was more like a community working together, and no one seemed to mind doing without.

I did not meet my husband, Howard C. Brady, until after the war. He was a Master Sergeant in the Army for three years, and served in England and in France. He was so patriotic and proud that he served for his country. Howard passed away March 13, 2004. We are so sorry that he did not get to see the WW II Memorial. Jean and I are very proud to be among the Rosies who helped in the WW II effort. May God bless our country and keep her safe. I fly our flag every day for Howard and our country.

SMALL TOWN GAL, BOMBER BUILDER

by Velores (Val) McLean Mosher Schroeder Jones
Coos Bay, Oregon

Val McLean Jones in 1942 (left) and in 2002

When I was a 22-year-old divorcee, my children and I lived with my parents in a small town in northern Michigan. My friends moved to the city to help in the war effort and wages were better, so I, too, followed.

In Detroit, I worked for Murray Corporation, making airplane parts. I was taught riveting while on the job. Transportation was bad, so I moved to Ypsilanti (near Detroit) and after six weeks, I worked at Willow Run Bomber Plant helping build the B-24 fighter bombers. In war times, one could not quit a defense plant to work at another without a six-weeks' wait. Between jobs, I worked as a waitress and lived with friends.

Working the second shift as a riveter at Willow Run, I was soon transferred to wiring on the instrument panels. All wires were color-coded to eliminate mistakes. We worked in teams of three. My teammates were two Kentuckian brothers. I did all the wiring in places where they could not get their larger hands. They treated me with respect and kept me entertained with stories of Kentucky and their "stills." I enjoyed their accents and different ways of explaining things. We got along well as a team and as friends.

Everyone was engrossed in doing their job well, hoping they were helping the war effort. As the partially-built bombers moved on along the conveyer belt, we would get out of the nose down the line from where we started, and walk back and climb the ladder into another. I lived at Willow Village, a temporary village across from the bomber plant, within walking distance. Buses ran frequently, but it was quicker to walk, avoiding congested traffic.

My experiences as Rosie the Riveter are irreplaceable. I have many fond memories, both happy and sad. It helped me think, appreciate, and take nothing for granted. It gave me a wonderful understanding of people I would not have had otherwise. Most of all, I learned confidence and liking myself. I also tasted Kentucky moonshine!!!

I was a small town girl in every sense of the word. I was left by my husband, so I lived with my parents and worked at the local State Hospital. My ex-husband joined the service, was captured, and was a prisoner for 39 months in Osaka, Japan. Upon liberation in 1945, we remarried, but that marriage didn't work out, either. We were not taught how to handle life with a prisoner-of-war experience.

In 1963, I married an old hometown friend. We spent 28 years together until he died of cancer and heart failure. I moved west to be with my only brother and met Melvin Jones. We have been married for 14 years and are still going strong. I am active in the computer club and have edited their newsletter for the past three years. I have also been an active volunteer for 20 years with RSVP.

HOW ARE YOUR SPLICES?
by Rozella Petersen Mock
Springfield, Oregon

Rozella Mock while working at Gowan Air Base in Boise, Idaho in the 1940's (left) and in 2003

Over and under, 1, 2, 3, and 4 goes in where 6 comes out! Thus goes the chant of a cable splicer. The year was 1942 and the United States was at war! I was working at Gowan Air Force Base in Boise, Idaho, having been assigned to the Accessory Department. My name is Rozella. On the base, because of my name, they began calling me Rosie the Riveter. However, I was a cable splicer, not a riveter!

I received my training in Eugene, Oregon, on Chambers Street where a former airport had been converted into shops to train potential wartime workers in various fields. Our first task was to make a clamp and a marlin spike. These were to be the tools of our trade and I was very proud of them and learned to enjoy the work. There were only five of us in the class and for six weeks our days were divided in half – one part spent with books, the other half with the cables. We became very adept at our work, putting out spliced cables of various sizes .

On the base, however, there were very few orders for cables. I and another girl, who had trained with me, were the only cable splicers on the entire base. She was also assigned to Accessories and our work consisted of cleaning carburetors and other small parts and also filling the planes with oxygen. Mostly B-17's flew into our base, but there were also some B-24's. We loved the B-17's, but considered the B-24's to be cumbersome, awkward, and ugly.

The oxygen tanks were loaded onto a trailer and pulled out to the plane with a tug. Girls were not allowed to drive, but my boss took it upon himself to let me drive out to the plane until he got caught! Then he went to bat for me and told the officials he saw no reason why I should not be allowed to drive, as I did as good a job as any man. From that time on, girls were issued tug licenses!

To service the plane, someone had to be inside watching the gauges while the other person stayed on the ground to open and close the valves. The opening on the planes were always some five feet off the ground, and ladders were never available, so it was usually the girl who was boosted up into the plane.

Every month we were required to change shifts, from days, swing, then graveyard. My husband of only a few months (we were married shortly before Pearl Harbor) also worked at the base. The midnight to 8:00 a.m. (graveyard) shift was always the most difficult. Oh, how hard it was to stay awake during those wee hours of the morning. Sleep during the day was virtually impossible, since we lived next door to a school for airplane motors.

Those were very impressive years of my life and gave me added confidence in entering the work world later on in life. I treasure the memories.

ROSIE THE RIVETER
by Cleo Evans Lorette
Sun City, Arizona

Cleo Evans Lorette in the 1940's

I was raised in Muskogee, Oklahoma, the second child and first daughter in a family of nine children. Even before graduation from high school, I worked for Dr. Grimm, an optometrist in Muskogee, for three years. There I met and married cattleman Ray Morton Lorette a month after Pearl Harbor and six months before he enlisted in the Air Force. World War II was already in full swing.

While Ray was in boot camp and awaiting assignment overseas, I took a course in aeronautics, and was one of the first three women. We were all between the ages of 20 and 24, and two had husbands in the service. We were assigned to work on the assembly line at Douglas Aircraft in Tulsa, Oklahoma. I worked there for one year as an hydraulic installer on the leading edge of the ailerons. The 4F's we worked with let us know we were invading their private territory. And they made no effort to change their vile language. They treated us like gofers until we began to fight back. Our leadman tried to control the sexual harassment, but had no laws to back him up.

Ray wrote he had been assigned to Engineering and it appeared he would not be going overseas, so would I like to come to cold Presque Isle, Maine? I didn't hesitate. Presque Isle, Maine was the jumping off place for soldiers headed for the European Theater of Operation.

I was given top secret clearance by the War Department and assigned to the Base Quartermaster's office as a secretary. When the North Atlantic Wing of the Air Transport Command moved to Manchester, New Hampshire, Ray and I were reassigned there. Ray worked in the Hoyt Building with Engineering and I worked across the hall in Priorities and Traffic. I was secretary to two colonels and one major.

After V-J Day, Ray was sent to the west coast to prepare for shipment to Japan as the Army of occupation. I continued to work for the War Department in Manchester until it became evident that Ray would not be sent to Japan. I joined Ray there and two months later, in April, 1946, Ray received an honorable discharge at the grade of Tech Sergeant.

Cleo Lorette

THE WAR OF A CENTURY
by Manuela A. Rojas
Phoenix, Arizona

Manuela Rojas at age 17 in the 1940's (left),
and at age 79 in 2004

It was a dream! When I graduated from high school I wanted to become a WAC and join the service.

My mother said no! So my dream was forgotten. I lived in El Paso, Texas, but one day my mother and all my seven siblings and I moved to California. Trying to find a job was hard, but I worked as a fruit vendor at the Central Market. I also worked at a Thrifty Drug Store, and at a winery called Morgan David. The pay was very little. I made friends with a girl that worked in a factory, assembling planes for the war and working the graveyard shift in Burbank, California.

She asked me if I wanted to work the graveyard shift, and I replied, "Yes, if the pay is better."

I had to work from around 7:30 p.m. to 8:00 a.m. First, I had to be trained. If I passed the training then I could work, and I did. I passed it with flying colors.

The training was for learning how to weld and solder and paint grind polish. It was also to learn how to install electrical wiring on the plane's engine. I also had to learn how to rivet the plates using hot and cold rivets on a P-38. I learned to use the air guns. It was not an easy job. We also had to learn how to maneuver ourselves on the tops of the skeleton planes.

The crews were mostly women. We had to wear bandanas, so our hair would not get caught in the machines and so we would not get scalped. We also wore aprons and heavy boots to protect us.

We were working with planes, but not just any planes, they were planes to fight the war. We helped to win WW II by holding down the home front, and we proved ourselves in a man's world. The importance of our job hit me like a punch in the stomach.

The skeletons were real planes flying to save the war. Before they left to fight our war, we installed pieces of paper with our names on them, and blessings for working to win the war.

One day there was stillness, and over the speaker, we heard that the war was over. We dropped our tools and ran outside. People were laughing and crying all at the same time. People in cars were honking their horns in joy. It was a very joyous day. Our soldiers were coming home.

I asked permission to go to El Paso to get our belongings. My mother passed away that same year.

I worked from 1942 to 1945. I am now 79 years old and live in Phoenix, Arizona. I am a volunteer and I help seniors like me. I also belong to the Holocaust Museum in El Paso, Texas. I designed Jewish boots, representing all the children that died.

FROM SCHOOLTEACHER AND MOTHER TO RIVETING INSTRUCTOR

by Ruth McEhaney Irvin
Phoenix, Arizona

Ruth McEhaney Irvin in 1941 (left) and in 2004

My life has been very blessed with countless adventures shared with my late husband in the academic, missionary, and diplomatic fields in the United States and overseas. Not too many people know, however, that while my husband, Fredric Irvin, was in the service during WW II, I was also doing my part as a "Rosie the Riveter," or, more accurately, as a riveting instructor.

Our baby, Sally, was a year old when Fred went into the service. One day in 1943, Fred's sister called me in Pennsylvania and said, "Why don't you come out to Cleveland and get a job working in the aircraft plant? I'll take care of the baby."

I said, "Well, if you think this will work. I don't know a soul out there except you folks." In addition to the prospect of helping the war effort, I found the pay attractive. I had been teaching school for $5 a day, and the job I eventually got paid $2 an hour.

After arriving in Cleveland, I filled out an application for riveters at the aircraft plant. About five minutes after I turned in my application, an officer came over to interview me. He said, "You're a teacher, aren't you?"

"Yes, I am," I replied, "and have been for seven years."

"We hope that you will be a good student, and if it works out we can make you an instructor of riveting," the officer said. "Don't tell anyone except your husband. When the training is over we'll see how you did."

I went home and called my husband at the base in Florida where he was stationed. I told no one else – not even my instructor – about the plans they had for me. It was hard work learning to countersink the rivets so that they were perfectly level with the surface. When we came to the end of the training, the rest of the students went out to work on the aircraft. I was the only one that was retained. The others thought that I had failed the course.

Once I started teaching, I had about eight students in each group. In one round of students, I had a man who, for some reason, was constantly grumbling and was very hard to deal with. I went to my former teacher and said, "What am I going to do with this man?"

"Nothing," he said. "He'll come to you in a few days. Just help him to get started and pay a little bit more attention to him than you've been giving him." That's exactly what happened. In the end, he had a very good record.

In general, there was not much lollygagging around and socializing like there is today. It was wartime, and we knew that we had a job to do. We started early in the morning, often after long bus rides to the plant. I got home around 3:30, took care of my baby, and went to bed early.

Looking back, I would say that this experience had a lot of influence on the rest of my life, though I did not necessarily realize the significance of it then.

MY CALL TO SERVE
by Freddella "Della" Iverson Fredricksen
Sun City, Arizona

Della Fredricksen in 1942 (left) and more recently

On December 7, 1941, I was attending college in St. Paul, Minnesota. It was Sunday and I attended church with friends. After church, we met in the activity room and turned on the radio and heard the terrible news of Pearl Harbor. It was terrible news, especially for the young men as the word of the draft was discussed.

I finished that year and started the next, but in October, I felt that I should be doing something for the war effort. I decided to quit school and go home to northern Minnesota, say good-bye to my parents, and go to California. I had traveled on trains many times before, but never a long three-day trip. Since it was war, the train was filled with young men on their way to the coast to training camps. We sat up all night. In the car where I was, there were troops from a parachute division. As I remember, it was orderly, with no drinking, etc. But they were long days.

The next stop was Ogden, Utah. They switched engines, but we stayed on the same car. One of the fellows gave me his parachute pin. I could never remember his name but it was a nice gesture. They seemed so young, even then. Going to California, we passed miles and miles of orange trees, the first I had ever seen.

I had two younger brothers. One had to stay on the farm to help my father, and the younger one quit school and joined the Merchant Marines.

Applying for a job at Lockheed was a new experience. First they wanted to see my birth certificate. I did not have one, so I contacted my parents and they found out that the doctor who was at my birth had never registered me, as he had been called to another state to help with the flu epidemic and never came back. But my parents had no trouble having one made, as many people had known me.

I was given a job right away. It was in a very big building, with machines and equipment I had never seen. I took the midnight to 7:00 a.m. shift. Starting that first night, a very friendly older girl took me under her wing and we became good friends, although we did not work together.

I already had a brother and a brother-in-law in California working for Lockheed and Northrup Aircraft. I was hired at Lockheed in Burbank as a trimmer. I had to trim the cowling that goes around the nose of the plane behind the propellers, such as on the B-52. The sections had to be trimmed exactly on the scribed lines. I became quite good at it and did that job for more than two years on the graveyard shift. It became clear that I needed a change and I decided to go back to college.

This was certainly a growing and learning experience for a young girl from a small Midwest town, but I did feel I had contributed to the war effort and had no regrets that I did it.

REMARKABLE ROXIE

by *Roxie Ott Turney*
Langley, Washington

Roxie Turney at age 25

In 1942, shortly after the Pearl Harbor attack, my husband joined the Coast Guard Military Police in Portland, Oregon. I decided to train at a machinist school so that I could help with the war effort. I learned how to run a lathe and a drill press. We had a live-in nanny to care for my two children, which freed me up to do the training.

After about a month, I qualified to work in an airplane parts factory in Portland. Employees were required to have a family member in the service. Not only was my husband serving, but also two brothers and a brother-in-law. We also had to be finger-printed at the local police station.

I was the second woman to go to work in this small,

but very secret, airplane factory. In order to get to work, I had to walk six blocks to a streetcar and travel over town, then I walked on the underground street to connect with another streetcar, which I rode to the end of the line. The factory was another two or three blocks from there. I worked from 7:00 a.m. to 5:00 p.m., ten hours a day, five days a week. I was 26 years old, and my earnings were about $42 a week.

One memory that stands out is the day that a beautiful young girl had an accident. She worked right next to me. She was from the Bronx and she wore her hair in the beehive style. I heard her scream and then I saw that she had caught her hair in the drill. I quickly turned off her machine and ran for help. They had to take the machine apart to repair it!

Many years later I had an extraordinary encounter with another fellow employee. This man was my neighbor and worked at the same plant. Until he joined the service, he often gave me rides to work. Around 1959, I was traveling by plane to Denver from Ohio. When I entered the doorway, there was my former neighbor. He was the pilot of the plane. We recognized each other and agreed that it is a small world indeed.

Roxie still loves to dance. Here she is in her black lace "fanny flapper" dance dress at age 84. She also volunteers weekly with Alzheimer's patients and at a local food bank and thrift store.

THE BATTLE OF SEATTLE
by LaPriel Frandsen Ash
Sun City West, Arizona

LaPriel Ash in the 1940's, as pictured on her Seattle Port of Embarkation identification card

After graduating from high school in 1942, I left Canada for school in Seattle, Washington. I soon discovered I could get a job at the Port paying $60 every two weeks.

I worked for a Major who supplied goods to our fighters in the Japanese war. We received trucks, jeeps, and other goods from the railroad and drove them to the port and loaded the ships. They sailed to Alaska and islands.

When our boys landed on Okinawa, we loaded a truck with beer. When it arrived, it was warm. The pilots took it up to 30,000 feet to cool it.

Our boss's son was in the service and asked if we would all write him a love letter. Ten boys had put in $10 each. The one who received the most love letters that month would get the $100. That's "American ingenuity."

We worked six days a week. I was happy to help the war effort a little, while others gave so much.

I hear the planes from Luke Air Force Base fly over and say, "Thank you, God, they are ours."

*LaPriel's identification card
from the Seattle Port of Embarkation*

MY WORLD WAR II EXPERIENCES
by Ginny Taylor
Sun City, Arizona

Ginny Taylor, welding a flange to an airplane body part

I lived on Long Island in New York. After an accident, I looked for a warmer climate and I decided to go to California. The war had already started and it took me three weeks to arrive in California, as the servicemen had priority on the Greyhound bus.

After a couple of days of rest, I walked around looking for a job and saw a sign reading, "Weldors wanted. $1.10 an hour to learn." (Note: A person is a "weldor" and the machine is a "welder.") I had never heard of such high wages. The lady at the desk explained what welding was. I didn't understand a thing she said, but I signed up for it.

The Maritime Commission trained and certified me as an Arc Weldor. I was hired at the California Shipyard in

Terminal Island, California. With a leather jacket, heavy steel-tipped shoes and a welding hood, I started working on Liberty boats, welding top decks, double bottoms, and tanks in 114 degree and more temperatures. Being a new employee, I got the work no one else wanted.

Some of the men did not like to see us women do as well as we did and gave us a bad time. We were very determined females, and for the love of our country we never reported the men urinating in the tanks where we had to weld while crawling in the double bottoms. The men would lower or mess up our machines and we had to crawl out, reset the machines, and lug the hoses through small openings and continue our work. I'm sure that after a while the men started to realize we were serious about our work and they started to be nice and helpful. Not many men were mean. Most were very nice and understanding.

After V-J Day, I moved to San Diego and took up heli-arc welding at San Diego Vocational School. I worked for Solar and Ryan Aircraft. Not having had much time with the company, I got laid off, so I went back to Long Beach, California. I was hired by McDonnell Douglas. Over the years I was certified in gas welding, which made me a combination weldor. I was also certified in heli-arc aluminum, stainless, titanium and silver braze, etc. I loved my work and retired on May 29, 1979 with 25 years of wonderful working experience.

I will be 84 this year and am proud of my willingness to have taken the abuse from some workers, though most of them — about 98% — were very helpful and grateful to us females.

God Bless America.

Ginny with Uncle Sam at Bell Recreation Center in 2004

FROM RIVETING TO DRIVING

by
Patricia J. Felton

Sun City West, Arizona

Patricia J. Felton

At age 21 and weighing a good 100 pounds, my riveting days of WW II were short. While I was employed at Tinker Air Force Base in Oklahoma City, I was selected to be transferred to Hickam Field in Honolulu, Hawaii. It was a lucky break. My riveting changed to driving. After the usual tests at the Motor Pool, I qualified to drive all extant Army vehicles except 2½ -ton trucks.

One of my first orders was to take a Lieutenant from Hickam Field up the side of a mountain to a radar station. There was no road. It was open, rough, rocky terrain. We made it. It was straight up the mountain in an Air Force Jeep.

For the two hours that I waited, I worried about driving down, down, down. It looked different from the top.

The Lieutenant returned with another passenger, a Warrant Officer, to join us. The Lieutenant sat in the front seat, the Warrant Officer in the rear. Off we started to the edge of the mountain.

Suddenly, I remembered: when going downhill, to control the gain, put the vehicle in second gear. I did. I put it into second after we were clipping down the mountain. Guess what? When I shifted into second and let out the clutch, I almost let out the officers, too – almost out of the Jeep! But we made it. At the bottom of the mountain, on the highway again, they mopped their brows, said, "Thanks, a good job," and signed my dispatch.

The same Lieutenant Hollingsworth asked for me again several days later. This time I was to take him around the island for another meeting. It was a lovely drive along the coast. The ocean was placid and blue and we chatted. That was going. On the return trip we came up behind a convoy of 2 ½-ton trucks loaded with GI's.

It is illegal to cut in on a convoy. The mountain road wound on for miles, single lane. Again, the Lieutenant needed to make it to another meeting fast. He decided I should go around the convoy. I prayed no car would be coming on this single lane road.

Remember, the ocean was on my left. I looked over the water. It was the shark-infested side of the island. I was going along fine until I saw a car coming toward us.

"Dodge in – in," the Lieutenant said. The GI's waved and yelled. I slipped in between the trucks until the car passed. Then I took off to the yells of "Made it! Good!"

I got the Lieutenant to his meeting on time. He was one happy passenger. As he signed my dispatch, he said, "Pat, you drive exactly like a New York cab driver." It was interesting and a compliment that he asked for me as his regular driver.

CHANGE ORDER
by Mary Crapster Dunham Nichols
Baltimore, Maryland

Mary Crapster with Betty Lippy Hopkins in 1943, and in her new wool suit in 1944

I was a senior at Glen Burnie High School in Maryland in the spring of 1943. A recruiter from Glenn L. Martin aircraft Company appealed to young women who had all the math and science courses they could take to help build bombers. I signed on.

I graduated in June, and had just turned 17. I rode the local train to Baltimore and walked to the War Housing Office. My interviewer offered to rent me her spare bedroom. I walked a few blocks to Johns Hopkins University, where for several months we young women recruits learned how to use a T-square, slide rule, pen and India ink without smearing, and a straight edge and ruler to precise measurements of 1/32, 1/64, and 1/128 inch.

When training was over, I worked in a Baltimore office building where Martin's occupied several floors. On the sixth floor, T. I. Schwartz manufactured uniforms. I wanted a suit. I chose a wool men's gray pinstripe material. I felt rich in my very first made-to-order three-piece suit with hat to match! I liked it so much Schwartz made me one in heather wool.

Later, Martin's moved our office to the main plant at Middle River, Maryland. I worked in Change Order on the B-26. To get there, I took a street car to North Avenue and rode a rickety bus to the plant where I worked six days one week, five days the next, changing vellum drawings for blueprints. On the way home, some of us would eat at the Oriole Cafeteria on North Avenue.

In the evenings I took typing and shorthand at a secretarial school in downtown Baltimore. I wanted a way to earn money as I worked my way through college after the war. I stood on the street corner at 10:00 p.m. two nights a week, waiting for my bus. Some weekends I rode the train home or spent it at a friend's home on a farm. I also went to parties at a Hopkins fraternity, where I met my future husband the semester before he joined the Navy.

Mary Nichols in 2003

The day after V-J Day, I resigned from Martin's, and soon enrolled at the University of Maryland. I graduated in 1949 with a degree in Early Childhood Education, and taught for 25 years.

I married my Naval Academy fiancé on June 4, 1950. Our daughter was born on August 29, 1951. He became MIA on October 7, 1952 in a Cold War shoot-down. I have been married to my present husband since 1965, and have a wonderful daughter and two special grandsons.

ROSIE JANE HELPS THE WAR EFFORT
by Jane Headrick Chason
Millbrook, Alabama

Jane H. Chason at age 79

I was living in Dutton, Alabama during WW II, at the tender age of 18, when I learned that if I went to welding school in Chattanooga, Tennessee and became a certified welder, the school would find me a job working in the shipyard in Savannah, Georgia. To me, this was a great way to help the war effort, and make a little money at the same time.

However, because I came from a large farming family,that, at that time, had only my widowed mother to support it, I did not have the $250 that it cost to go to school – a great deal of money by any standards in 1942. Fortunately, I knew the Postmaster, Rosey Cauthen, pretty well, and I asked her if I could borrow the $250. She graciously loaned me the money. I know that there were many girls my age, that had been given the opportunity to make something of their lives, and I was extremely grateful for mine. After I got out of school, I did in fact find work at the shipyard, and was able to honor my debt to Ms. Cauthen, making payments over the next several months.

For two years, I welded on what was known as the "second shift," 3:00 p.m. to 11:30 p.m. I would routinely work five, six, or even seven days a week. Being 5' 2" and weighing 100 pounds, I was always placed in close quarters to weld, and that was in the bow of the ship. It was certainly hard work, and I was always soaked with perspiration, but the work was very satisfying.

In order for people to keep their jobs at the yard, they had to retain their welding rod tips, and then trade them in for new ones. No tips meant no more work. So if you ever found a rod tip, you put it in your pocket to take the place of any that you may have lost.

As the war went on, I moved on to Mobile, Alabama, where I got a job at the Greyhound bus station and became a counter clerk.

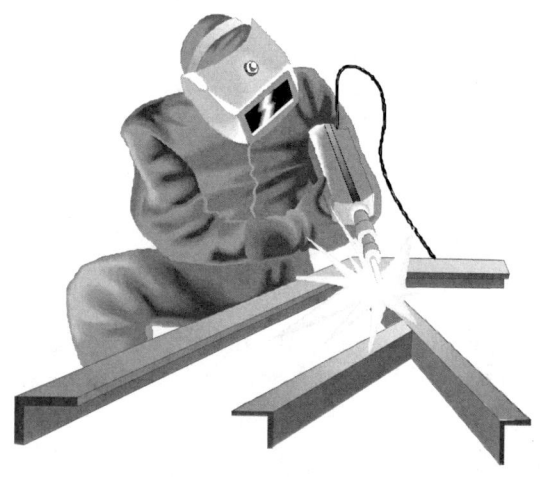

FROM HAWAII, DECEMBER 7, TO V-J DAY, CHICAGO

by
Dr. Joan Stidham Nist

Auburn, Alabama

Joan Stidham Nist as a junior at Leilehua High School in 1941

In 1940 and 1941, living in Hawaii, I volunteered at the local Red Cross like many schoolmates. We made bandages for Britain, half a world away, and we took first aid courses to earn extra PE credit.

Then, on the first Sunday of December, as we prepared for church, we looked down the hill from Wahiawa Heights to see the bombardment of Wheeler Field, air base of the Army's large Schofield Barracks. One of the attacking planes flew our way, machine-gunning nearby hen houses mistaken for barracks, flying so low over us that we saw the pilot in his helmet and goggles, and worse – the rising sun emblem on the plane wings.

At first there was fear of more attacks and invasion. Very soon came martial law, nightly blackouts, fuel rationing, the first mass fingerprinting of a U.S. population, obligatory ID cards and gas masks – relics from WW I, ugly, heavy, smelly. Christmas was not *mele* but bleak; letters were censored and slow, sent by ship for there was little commercial air traffic.

Then we received three-day notice that we could be on the tense 10-day, 9-ship convoy back to the Mainland. Our overcrowded, converted liner had little fresh water, no milk for the many evacuated children aboard, and at the end, spoiled meat. The Golden Gate Bridge was never more beautiful than seen from below on that March, 1942 day. The Red Cross met us with warm hand-knit sweaters to supplement our light Hawaiian clothes.

I returned to high school in the Chicago area that spring. We students volunteered to give out recruiting and war stamp/bond information and collected recyclable things, from toothpaste tubes to foil gum wrappers. At college, I chaired the War Board, organizing the recycling. Summers, I qualified as a soldering, rather than a riveting, Rosie at Mossman Company, a manufacturer of small metal components for war material on the outskirts of Chicago. With gas rationing keeping highway traffic down, I could bike the mile back and forth to work.

The summer of 1945, I worked for the Army Department of Transportation at Union Station in downtown Chicago, where we routed returning soldiers from Europe onto trains west for the push against Japan. One mid-August day, my folks came downtown to meet me, and so it was that with them I was on the people-filled streets of the "Loop" to celebrate V-J Day.

Joan in 2003, a lecturer for the Alabama Humanities Foundation on the topic, "Eyewitness: Hawaii, Dec. 7, 1941"

THEY CALLED ME "JOSIE THE RIVETER"
by Josephine Binelli Paddock
Mannsville, New York

*Josephine Paddock
in the 1940's*

When America entered WW II, my husband worked for the GLF Petroleum Company in Hudson, New York. The Athens Shipyard across the Hudson River was hiring women riveters. I was hired as a riveter on steel lifeboats. I walked to the ferry to cross the Hudson River to the shipyard to work. This was from 1941 to 1942.

The boats were shaped on wooden forms in a bottoms-up position. Small women were needed because we had to crawl through a small opening and rivet for eight-hour days. Men too old to serve bucked the rivets on the outside. We were paid $32 per week, and each week I purchased a war bond. My name being Josephine, I've been called Josie the Riveter.

One day I decided that it was unfair that the men were receiving more pay per hour than we were, so I called the girls together. We decided that we should all walk out at a given hour. We did, and we got our raise. We also asked that a sign lettered "Colored" be removed from a restroom door.

My husband enlisted in the Navy in Hudson, New York, and left for San Diego. I cashed in the war bonds and with my two-year-old son, I left for San Diego. My son amused the travelers on the train singing "Bell Bottom Trousers." We were happy to spend six months with my husband before he left for Guam. We returned to our home in Adams, New York, and waited for his return here in 1946.

Pounding rivets for eight hours a day left me with a hearing loss. I learned from my work as a riveter at the Athens Shipyard that you should take a stand against unfair and abusive treatment. Along the way I've helped others to do the same.

Josephine in 2003

MY DAYS AS ROSIE THE RIVETER
by Lena England Ryan
Ashville, Alabama

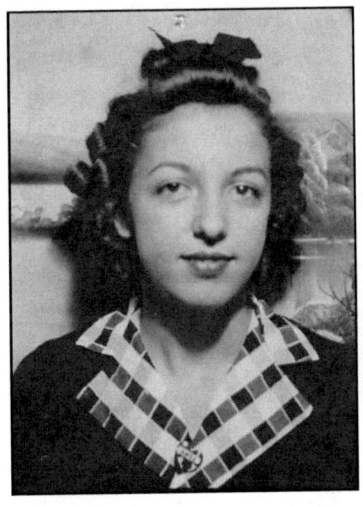

Lena England Ryan at age 23

In 1941, I married Oscar Stanley, my childhood sweetheart. He was in the Army, having volunteered in February of 1940. Shortly after our marriage, he was sent to Europe. I moved from Tennessee to Alabama and went to work at Bechtel McCombs Parsons Airplane Plant. I worked there until 1945. During that time, my husband was killed. I continued working in the defense plant until the plant closed in 1945.

I was a riveter, and I also bucked rivets. The bomber we worked on – the B-29 – was something to behold. It had a wing span of 141 feet. I would get at the tip of one wing and run up and over the body of the plane to the other wing tip. I did this quite often just because I wanted to. I worked on the life rafts, the two gun turrets, and on the front of the plane. I was called on by the roving crew to buck rivets, at times hanging high in the air in a swing. I signed off on one of the planes saying, "Lena worked here." Some time later I received a letter from the crew thanking me for a job well done. The letter stated that they had made several successful missions so as a result, they felt I gave them luck. They named their plane "Leaping Lena." I saw this on the newsreel at the Alabama Theater about a month later. This pleased me very much. I feel honored to have helped my country by working on the biggest and fastest bomber of WW II.

In 1947, I married Claude Ryan, a veteran who fought in the Pacific. We have two daughters, who are ARRA Rosebuds. After 54 years of marriage, my husband died on May 18, 2001.

I have a ring that was made for me from a B-29 bolt. The ring is inlayed with gold and is engraved with my name on it. I'm very proud to have served my country in my small way.

Lena at age 83

OUR WARTIME HEROINE

by
Barbara Burkhardt Landry and Joseph Burkhardt, Jr.

Children of Mae Burkhardt

New Orleans, Louisiana

Mae Archibald Burkhardt with her husband, Joe, and daughter, Barbara, about 1941, New Orleans, Louisiana

The earliest memory I have of my mother, Mae Burkhardt, working was when my brother and I must have been around three and four years old, in 1944. My aunt, Ruby Tauzin, and my cousin, Ella Fortner, were staying with us while El's husband, Henry, was in Galveston, Texas with the Naval Coast Guard. I remember my mother and Ella leaving our house in their gabardine slacks and shirts with a bandana tying their hair up – much like the picture of the wartime female worker that is so popular.

Aunt Ruby stayed with the two of us while my mother worked the evening shift at Consolidated Aircraft on Lake Ponchartrain. My father worked at Delta Shipyard on the Industrial Canal.

My brother and I would listen to the stories my mother and cousin would tell after a day's work. We didn't quite understand some of the stories until we were older.

Years later, after our mother and cousin had ended their careers as Rosie the Riveters, they would get together and exchange stories. They spoke of the faulty, or not well-grounded equipment (drills, drill presses, etc.) which would sometimes cause them to be "stuck" to it. I guess they were receiving a small shock, and the power would have to be turned off by another worker for them to be released. They also talked of the "activities" that sometimes went on in the planes. When they'd get a plane almost finished, some of the men and girls would get up in them and play around.

There was one plane – a PBY5a – that, when put in the water for a test, it sank! The workers had paid less attention to what they were doing and more attention to each other! We also remember them talking about a community of "little people" who lived close to the plant and worked in the small areas of the planes where no one else could get.

Our mother was a riveter at Consolidated for about a year. When the plant work was going to move to California, Mother was offered a job with them, but she didn't accept.

We are very proud of our mother's and cousin's support of the war effort, and we know she would have been pleased to be a part of the American Rosie the Riveter Association.

THE BLIND RIVETER

by
Kathleen Sherrow

Tecumseh, Kansas

Kathleen in 2004 - truly in the Rosie spirit!

What were you doing when news of Pearl Harbor came? I was bumping a pinball machine at the Maryville, Missouri Lunch Box, trying to win enough points for a free hamburger, all for the price of a nickel. No money was exchanged, and there are not machines like that today.

I was hesitant about leaving my job after high school. However, Morton Aircraft's ad promising better pay and an opportunity to serve our country won.

A baseball friend and I went for the training and became a blind-riveting team. After graduation, Morton placed us with United Airlines in Cheyenne, Wyoming, repairing aircraft being damaged in combat. Sometimes, as you viewed the blood stains and bullet holes, you felt you were close to the war zone. One B-17 Flying Fortress was estimated to have 500 bullet holes.

Once, while repairing a B-17, I saw a girl crawling

over the top gun turret. I turned it a wee bit, and she let out a scream that echoed that metal building. I realized, a little too late, that this was a dangerous thing to do. Fortunately, my apologies were accepted.

There were no living quarters in Cheyenne, so old school buses transported us for 25 cents a day. After experiencing a bus breakdown in a blizzard, we had word from a Lockheed employee that women would be hired for the mechanized line. On December 7, 1942, we were hired, some of the first on the line. Group leaders were not overjoyed, and gave us some tough assignments, such as attaching empennages and fitting cabin doors. Having riveted as a team, we were able to produce. My friend became an Inspector and I brought up the motor controls in the cockpit of P-38's. We didn't realize how much we were appreciated until we were pulled from our jobs and moved to Experimental, to assist in getting the Constellation on schedule.

Katie at a Rosie the Riveter convention in Arizona in 2002. In 2003, she was Inducted into Topeka's Park and Recreation Hall of Fame.

My dad had a damaging stroke, so I resigned on May 3, 1945. After Dad's death on June 11, 1945 at the age of 52, I worked at Pratt Whitney Aircraft in Kansas City until the war ended. Now I find myself again thinking, "What can I do to help bring peace to our nation?"

A CENTENARIAN ROSIE

by
Nellie Rains Pringle

Maryville, Missouri

As told to her niece,
Kathleen Sherrow

I am not a "youngun" anymore, as I celebrated my 100th birthday on June 2, 2002. There were 42 present to cheer me as I stepped out of a limousine. Many of my 22 nieces and nephews were there to greet me. As cameras were flashing, I said, "Why didn't you have a handsome young man ride with me?"

I am the youngest of twelve children so, consequently, much sadness has touched my life, to have grandparents, parents, husband, all my siblings, and many nieces and nephews depart. However, much joy has come by having many relatives.

Again at the Rains Family Reunion on October 6, 2002, a tribute of "This Is Your Life" was given me. 2002 was my year for celebration. Another highlight came in June, 2002, when my niece, Kathleen Sherrow, attended the national convention of ARRA in Surprise, Arizona, and I was advised that I was eligible to be a "Rosie the Riveter." My eligibility came from my working at the Naval Gun Factory in Washington, D. C., where I made range finders for the ships' guns. I worked from 1942 until my marriage on August 22, 1945 to James Pringle. Then I went back to the life most appealing to me – the farm life.

I worked side by side with my husband during all planting and harvesting. It was difficult to leave it all behind when my husband of 47 years passed away. My nieces and nephews came to my rescue, working five days in preparation for a two-day auction. The farm sold, and with a few of my cherished possessions, including over 200 genealogy books, The Chateau assisted living apartment in Maryville, Missouri, became my new home in June, 1992.

In 1999, I fell and had to have a hip pinned, then six weeks in rehabilitation. At age 97, that was my first admittance to a hospital and, fortunately, my only surgery. In November 2002, the doctor told me, "I'll see you next spring." I feel blessed! I am happy to be an American and have tatted several U. S. flags. I feel honored to be a part of the American Rosie the Riveter Association, and one of its oldest members.

Editor's note: In the fall of 2004, as this book was being prepared for publication, Nellie R. Pringle passed away at the age of 102. At the time of her death, she was ARRA's oldest living member.

B-29 A REALITY
by Ann Lewis Doebbeling
Ness City, Kansas

*Anne Lewis Doebbeling
in the 1940's and in 2002*

The B-29 Superfortress bomber was authorized to Boeing in Wichita, Kansas in February, 1940. In May, 1944, I graduated from high school and boarded a train for Wichita to join my sisters, Ethel, Beulah, and Betty, who were already working in defense plants. My brother, Charles, was in the Navy, stationed in Europe, and my brother, James, was in the Army in the south Pacific.

The day after my arrival in Wichita, I secured a job at Boeing. I was sent to the Division of Aircraft Training on North Waco at 65 cents per hour. Blueprints and bucking rivets were "my thing." In a short time, I was bucking rivets at Boeing. Getting to work cost a nickel to ride a bus downtown and a dime for a bus to the plant.

This small-town country girl was overwhelmed by the size of the Boeing plant. I was instructed to get off the bus at a designated ramp. Guards were stationed at the entrance. My identification number and picture were pinned to my blouse. I entered a long, never-ending tunnel where I clocked in. I arrived in a wide-open area where five B-29's were being assembled. The noise made verbal communication impossible, and there was no end that I could see. My knees began to buckle, my tool box became heavy, and I felt "so small."

I was introduced to my partner and checked out three different bucking bars from a nearby tool bin. I stepped into this enormous skeleton part of a plane enclosed with sheet metal. In a short time, my partner taught me the necessary signals and I loved my job.

I was eventually transferred to the Electrical Wiring Department 222. Marty Clawson from Cheney, Kansas was my partner. We took turns operating a machine that stamped the correct ID numbers on wires, while the other rolled them into neat bundles. We prided ourselves as being the fastest snd most efficient machine operators. We both thrived on challenge and were loaned out to different departments when our work was completed. At this time I was earning $1.15 per hour, plus overtime. I purchased one $25 bond each month.

After getting off work at 4:00 a.m. I often went roller skating. I enrolled in swimming lessons at the YWCA for 25 cents a lesson. My sisters and I rented bicycles on Sunday afternoon and were members of the Shadow Land Dance Club. I learned patience standing in a two-block line to see a movie or a three-block line to get a single pair of nylon hose.

Many friendships were formed during those years, but I would never want the war years to be repeated. The B-29 long-range bomber proved to be decisive in the Pacific war. I am happy and feel very fortunate to have played a part during that era.

DOROTHY GOES TO THE CITY

by
Dorothy Hopper Martin

Port Orchard, Washington

Dorothy and Robert Martin on their wedding day in November, 1944, North Hollywood, California

In 1942, I left Billings, Montana, and came to the big city of Seattle, Washington to work for the Boeing company. At the age of 22, I was considered a "country bumpkin." I worked in Plant 2 as a tool checker in the Transportation Department. My job involved making sure all the correct tools were loaded on these large carts, and also to transport tools from one shop to another.

Since Montana is known for its sheep ranches, there were times I was given some good-natured teasing by the few men who worked there. Whenever I would wear my soft leather vest to work, they would say, "Hey, lambie-pie, when are you going b-a-a-a-ck to Montana?"

There were many things we had to do without, but we were happy to sacrifice anything for our servicemen. As nylons were scarce, we would use leg makeup, and have a girlfriend draw the "seam" down the back of our legs with an eyebrow pencil.

I also remember the day the President of the United States (FDR) came to visit the plant. He was quite a handsome man riding in his convertible. We all had to stand in line as he drove by. It was a real thrill to see him up close.

I transferred to Lockheed in Burbank, California a couple of years later. That's where I met and married a sailor! We had only known each other a couple of weeks and went out on one date. The Navy Chaplain tried talking us out of getting married because some women were marrying servicemen, hoping they wouldn't come back so they could collect on their life insurance. We had 51 wonderful years together before he passed away in 1995. From that union we have three children, five grandchildren, and eight great-grandchildren that are a very important part of my life.

The war years were a time for lots of happy memories, but sad ones, also.

Dorothy in 2004

FROM FARM FIELD TO AIRFIELD
by Frances Smith Wilkins
Vance, Alabama

AIRCRAFT MECHANIC CLASS
UNIVERSITY OF ALABAMA
1943

I had just turned 17 when the Japanese attacked Pearl Harbor on December 7, 1941. The next October I was 18 and by then, women were being recruited to do war work. I applied for Civil Service and was accepted in March of 1943 to train as an aircraft mechanic. Most of my classmates were women, some as old as my mother. Our training took place at the University of Alabama campus, where we had several kinds of airplanes to work on. From farm work to working on an airplane was a giant step for me.

After about four months of training, we were sent to Brookley Field at Mobile, Alabama (now Brookley Conference Center). I had never been away from home and it was a great adventure for me. We worked mostly on C-47 transports. I started out splicing cables for parachute ripcords, then was sent out on the line to install glider tow release cables in the C-47's. Gliders were used to get personnel and supplies behind enemy lines.

I also did maintenance work, removing the fuel tanks from the wings of C-47's to install new fuel lines. We had to crawl inside of the wings to remove the old lines and install new ones. Women were usually good at that kind of work, because they were usually smaller and more agile than men.

Some planes came in that had been hit by anti-aircraft fire and needed to be repaired. British planes were sent to us for maintenance and repair, and service men from Britain were sent to Brookley for aircraft maintenance training. That was my first experience with foreigners.

The *Memphis Belle* came on a bond drive. The crew lined up on the wings and talked to us about the importance of our work. Fifty years later, I went to Mud Island at Memphis and saw the old girl on display.

As Civil Service employees, we were housed in government dormitories. There were six bunks to a room, and it was very much like Army barracks. There was no privacy. We ate at the base cafeteria most of the time and were under the supervision of the Commanding Officer at Brookley Field.

The main lobby was used for recreational activities. The juke box was always going and it was a gathering place for soldiers looking for a dance partner or someone to talk to. Everyone seemed to be having fun, but in the back of our minds we knew that when they shipped out, some of them would never come home. Many of them didn't.

I am proud of my service that helped to "KEEP 'EM FLYING!"

THE EARLY YEARS
by Mary T. Stoutamire
Dowling Park, Florida

Left: Mary Taliaferro Stoutamire (far right) with co-workers in 1945. Right: Mary in 2003.

I was 14 or 15 when WW II began. I was attending high school in Blakely, Georgia at the time. I remember as if it were yesterday when my teacher, Mrs. Frances Balkcum, asked the class, "Who would like to join the NYA (National Youth Association)?" The government had asked everyone to be patriotic and help with the war efforts. I was one of the first to raise my hand as high as the sky. Mrs. Balkcum said we would need $8.00 to pay for the train ride to Atlanta, and then to Carrollton, Georgia. I was so excited. I had never ridden a train before.

When I went home that day, I never expected my parents to say no. But they did. They said, "You're too young to go." After crying and begging, I heard my father say to my mother, "Willie, give her the $8.00. She won't eat or sleep until you do." I was so happy! I filled out the form and attached the $8.00. Now I was on my way, from the flaming heat of the cotton fields to the fire of the bustling city.

    I can remember getting off the train in Atlanta on Peachtree Street. There was a lamppost made out of mirrors and I wrapped my arms around it. When I looked up, it began to snow. I was so happy to be there. While training in Carrollton, we stayed at an Army barracks and had to wear blue coveralls. I tried welding and several other jobs in a hangar filled with B-29's and P-38's. I machined valves, worked on the assembly line, put bearings in rocker-arms, and ordered parts for all the foremen. I worked on some planes that had returned from the war, damaged.

    After a few months, I had the opportunity to transfer to a town near my home of Arlington, Georgia. I chose Macon. While there, I took a Civil Service test and with only a tenth grade education, I passed. After that, I was sent to Robins Air Force Base. My main job was putting rivets in the wings of the airplanes, along with doing the other things I had learned while in Carrollton. I sent my mother a $25 war bond every month.

    When the war ended in 1945, they began to lay people off. I eventually resigned and became a telephone operator in Macon, Georgia. After about six months, my sister, Laura, told me that friends of hers, who owned the Cove Hotel in Panama City, Florida, were looking to hire a manager for the dining room. I met with the owners and got the job. I was trained for a multitude of tasks to run the dining room. At only 25 years of age, I had a lot of responsibility.

    After working at the Cove Hotel for about one year, I was invited to go with one of the owners' daughters-in-law to a big reunion. That is where I met the man who was to become the father of my children. And that's another story.

EIGHTEEN
by Frankie Jane LaField Collier
Oklahoma City, Oklahoma

Frankie LaField Collier and her mother, Martha LaField, going to work at Douglas Aircraft Company in August, 1944

Coming of age during WW II was not very difficult. When the war started, everyone became very patriotic and all of us wanted to do whatever we could to help. The devastation of Pearl Harbor and the death of our military men were on the minds of all of us. Our country asked for our help and we were there to give it without question.

In 1943, my mother was working for Douglas Aircraft Company in Oklahoma City as a riveter on the wing section of the C-47 planes they were building. On my eighteenth birthday, August 7, 1944, I went to the employment office of Douglas, took a typing test, and was hired as an inspection clerk. I had been working at the 5 & 10 store for $11 a week. My first check from Douglas was for $44 and I thought I was rich!

My desk was in Department 552, where they put the fuselage onto the wing of the plane. It was the most exciting place to watch the plane being finished and ready to fly.

We had to wear slacks and sturdy leather shoes to work. Slacks were a new thing for women! During the war, many things were rationed. We had to have a coupon in order to buy leather shoes. By the time you had enough money for the shoes, you had the coupon.

We did not have a car, so we paid another worker so we could ride with her and two other workers. One night, during the winter, when we got off work at 11:00 p.m., a terrific snow storm had started. The storm was so intense that the driver had to put her head out of the window to see. Needless to say, it was a very scary time!

We lived in a garage apartment that had a living room with a bed, a bedroom, a shower, and a small kitchen. For a short time, my cousin, Nina Bickerstaff, lived with us. We worked the swing shift, which was 3:00 to 11:00 p.m. So it was late at night by the time we got home, ate something, and went to bed.

Life was routine as we worked six days a week. We had one day to buy groceries, go to the beauty shop, and do other necessary errands. We did not have a telephone, but we had a small radio to listen to the war news. We worked until August, 1945, when the war ended and Douglas stopped building planes and became part of Tinker Air Force Base.

Frankie with Colonel Kathy Close at a luncheon honoring Rosies and other workers at Tinker Air Force Base in Oklahoma City.

MY CONTRIBUTION TO THE WORLD WAR II EFFORT
by June Midkiff Tinker
Waverly Hall, Georgia

June Midkiff Tinker (left) and two ladies with whom she roomed and carpooled in Springfield, Ohio, 1942-43

I was born in Coal City, West Virginia on July 13, 1925, to Ed and Josie Midkiff. My father was a coal miner and also a veteran of WW I. I well remember the years of the Great Depression, and couldn't imagine at that time enjoying the things I have now. But because of the sacrifices made during the wars (my brother, Kenneth, made that sacrifice on March 14, 1945 on Iwo Jima), we are still a free America. My mother was a school teacher until she started her own family, and soon she had nine pupils of her own.

My contribution to the war effort started when I was a junior in high school in Seth, West Virginia. It was 1942, and my two older brothers, Kenneth and Jake Midkiff, had joined the Marines soon after the war started. I had no idea the sacrifice they were making or would make before the war ended. But I felt a pulling in my heart to get into the action in some way. I was only 16, and the requirements were that you had to be 17 before you were qualified to join the National Youth Administration.

As soon as I had my seventeenth birthday, I left home for Charleston, West Virginia, where I spent several weeks learning to weld and type. I enjoyed this time of learning and making new friends. Times were hard at home due to the Depression, so the food in the mess hall was wonderful. It was the best food I had ever tasted, and I couldn't understand how some criticized it. Even though I quit school to get into this, I never doubted my decision. I got my GED when I was in my forties.

Soon I was working in Patterson Air Field, near Dayton, Ohio. I never used my welding training, however, but was retrained to be a riveter on the building of B-29 bombers. We worked three different shifts. I was on the second shift, which was fine with me. When rotation time came, I was on the midnight shift and I well remember how sleepy I got before the night was over. During some of the time I worked at Patterson Field, I used my typing training and helped out with filing and general office procedures.

My sister, Hope, and I rode to work in car pools and we would sing or listen to the radio during this time. I can still remember with joy those rides and the songs. Sometimes I sing them now, at nursing homes, where I entertain a couple of times a week. Those folks remember, too, and many sing along with me.

June entertaining at a nursing home, Columbus, Georgia, 2004

WORLD WAR II INFLUENCE ON MY LIFETIME CAREER
by Dorine Smith Hamilton
Wichita, Kansas

Dorine Smith Hamilton (left) and her sister, Elaine Smith O'Quinn, in 1943

I went to Wichita in 1941 and married in June, 1942. We joked that they flew the flags in honor of our anniversary. My husband went into the Army in November, 1942. I went to riveting school and took the first job offered to me at Boeing Airplane Company: handformer in the hydro press area. The Rosies need parts to have something to rivet! In 1943, my sister, Elaine, went to the same riveting school and became a riveter at Boeing. We worked the second shift with hours 4:45 to 3:30.

It was a "sorry" life for four years as a twenty-something, made livable by parents, siblings, and letters from my husband. In four years, I saw him for a few days twice, when he traveled from California to Fort Knox, Kentucky for mechanic training. He was home on leave when the war ended, as the 13th Armored had returned from Europe to train to go to Japan. We were stationed at Lompoc, California until he had enough points for discharge.

We returned to Wichita to live and work. He worked as a mechanic and I was a typist at Dun and Bradstreet and the Veterans Administration. My employment with the Defense Department started with the Air Force (civilian) at Boeing Airplane Company in 1954. In 1975, our office, where I was working as a production clerk, announced an upward mobility job opening with the requirement of experience in contractor production. I was the only one qualified. Hello!! My four years in Boeing Production!!

Here we find the outstanding influence of my four years in Boeing Production on my lifetime career, as it took me to Grade Seven. I later received other promotions. I retired at age 72 as a Grade Eleven Property Administrator. Thus the end of a lifetime career of 38 credit years with the federal government (Veterans Administration and the Department of Defense).

*Dorine Hamilton
in 2004*

PISTOL PACKIN' MAMA

by
Joyce Pistole Barrett

Sun City, Arizona

Joyce Pistole Barrett as she appeared in the Childress Army Air Force Base newsletter in the fall of 1943

What's in a name? DYNAMITE, that is, if you have the right name at the right time and you are in the right place. My maiden name just happened to be the name of a popular song in 1943, and I just happened to be noticed by an Air Force photographer.

In January 1943, as "Joyce Pistole," I became a Civil Service employee at the Childress Army Air Force Base, Childress, Texas. I was hired as a secretary in the Base Supply Office building and became the "right-hand girl" for Mr. Byron Bonner, who was responsible for the hundreds of orders for needed airplane parts. I searched parts manuals, checked and double-checked order numbers, and typed purchase orders. Every day I was reminded of the necessity of accuracy and the importance of expediency. I was a

"Rosie the Riveter" doing my small task to help in the war.

Like the story of the chicken and the egg, I don't know which came first – the Supply Staff Sergeant or the Photographer Staff Sergeant. Either way, I was selected as the Childress Air Force Base "Girl of the Week." As I sat behind my desk with my name plate, JOYCE PISTOLE, facing the entrance of the Supply Office, I was approached by the two service men who asked me for an interview and for permission to take my picture. Being young and naïve, of course, I agreed to this extra attention and was very excited to receive this recognition.

The following week, the CAAF newspaper was printed and distributed throughout the Base. From that time on, I became well-known as "Pistol Packin' Mama." Needless to say, I encountered a few jealous remarks from co-workers.

The Supply Staff Sergeant, Hugh S. Barrett, returned a few days after the interview, perched himself upon my desk, asked me for a date, and the rest is history. We were married on October 4, 1944, and celebrated 54 years together before his death on April 10, 1999.

I worked at the Childress Army Air Force Base until October, 1945 when the war ended and my husband received his discharge. During my employment, I met many patriotic, hard-working people – servicemen as well as civilians. I made many friends and developed some long-time friendships. I am proud to have been a "Rosie the Riveter" and performed my duty as a war-time employee.

Joyce Barrett as she appeared in the Sun Health Foundation newsletter in 2004

MY EXPERIENCE AS A ROSIE

by
Irene M. Hill

Oklahoma City, Oklahoma

Irene Marie Hill in the 1940's

I worked at the Douglas plant in Oklahoma City – Building 3001, which is now Tinker Air Force Base – from 1942 to August 1945, when WW II ended.

We built the C-47 cargo planes. I worked on the monorail, in Prime Paint, Department 454. I hung small parts on the rail, which went around, dipped them in paint, and then came back around with dried parts. One had to work pretty fast, putting on and removing parts, as the rail moved fairly fast. Larger parts were spray-painted.

I had been earning $24 a week as manager of a coffee shop in downtown Oklahoma City when the call came out for defense workers. At Douglas the pay was $1 per hour, or $40 weekly. We were paid time and a half for Saturday and double time for Sunday. I worked a 54-hour week for 6 months, without a day off.

Everyone wore a badge and we went through security guarded gates to enter our building. In those days most of us rode the bus, as not everyone had a car. Also, tires and gasoline were rationed. If we didn't get out of work fast, we had to stand in the bus all the way into Oklahoma City. One day on the way in, we received word that our President, FDR, had died in Warm Springs, Georgia. It was quite a blow.

We were required to wear slacks to work, so actually that was the beginning of women wearing trousers. It also contributed to more women working outside the home.

My husband was in military service, so I wanted to do what I could to help the war effort, as well. I am proud to have served our great nation. It was quite an experience. After the Douglas plant closed, many ladies went home to raise families. I went on to Tinker AFB.

Irene in 2004

AN OKLAHOMA ROSIE
by Donna Carpenter Highsmith
Austin, Texas

Donna Carpenter Highsmith (left) and Wanda Dickey take a break while repairing aircraft at Hickham Field on Oahu, Hawaii, 1944

I went to work for the federal government after graduating from high school in Wapanucka, Oklahoma in 1941. My local newspaper and radio broadcasts provided information regarding jobs for men and women. The federal government offered specialized training with hourly pay to all qualified applicants. Initially, I was sent to school to learn how to weld.

Upon completing my training, I was transferred to Tinker Air Depot, Oklahoma City. Upon my arrival, I was trained in aircraft mechanics for all Air Force bombers, such as the B-17, B-24, B-25, B-29, and some transport planes. My duties involved complete aircraft maintenance, such as repairing engines, and replacing and riveting sheet metal panels damaged in war. In 1943, I was transferred to Hickham Field on Oahu, Hawaii. I loved my job, and I felt very lucky to be earning an above-average income.

I worked side by side with men and women. I never experienced any animosity because of my gender. The men were very helpful toward the women on their crew. Everyone was given pay raises according to merit. However, men were given the positions of leadership. It was customary for men to fill these roles, and the women seemed to accept it.

Before WW II, women held domestic jobs such as being homemakers, nurses, and secretaries. After the war, women were able to pursue new positions in the workforce, including leadership roles. We were unaware that we were paving the road for the future of women. We were proud of our country and proud of our contribution for America.

I continued to work after the war until 1947, when I met and married my husband, Shelby H. Highsmith, a Navy officer stationed in Hawaii. We have two daughters and now reside in Austin, Texas. I am very proud to say I am a "Rosie the Riveter."

Donna in 2004

JUST MARRIED FOUR MONTHS

by Gladys Marley Jayme
Banning, California

Gladys Marley Eckels (now Jayme) with her husband of four months, George W. Eckels, in 1941

We graduated from high school in 1940, and married in August, 1941, four months before Pearl Harbor Day. We had just borrowed money for a down payment on a house, located about a mile from Douglas Aircraft Plant in Long Beach, California. My cousin lived with us for room and board, to repay our debt to him.

We all three went to work at the plant, but soon they were drafted. My cousin joined the Navy and became a pilot. My husband joined the Air Force and was later stationed in Okinawa. I moved back with my parents.

My mother, Hazel Marley, and I worked as a team. She

was the riveter and I bucked rivets from the other side of the bulkhead on the B-17 bombers. It was on-the-job training. The inspector would come around and if the rivets weren't in perfectly, we would have to drill them out and redo them. We were on our feet all day, sometimes crawling into tight places carrying a heavy rivet gun, bucking bar, or drill.

When the whistle blew at noon, we would stop and eat, usually at the spot where we were working. I remember a black lady always brought a sweet potato sandwich. My mother thought that was so great, she started taking sweet potato sandwiches, too.

After work at night, sometimes there were blackouts. We would turn out the lights, put blankets on the windows, and light candles.

I worked about a year, then followed my husband from base to base, working at the PX on the Army bases. After the war, I went back to work at McDonnell Douglas (formerly Douglas Aircraft), this time in the office. I am now retired.

Currently my daughter, Diane Storms, is co-owner of a construction management company for the schools in southern California, and a member of NAWIC (National Association of Women in Construction). I am proud to be a "Rosie" and my daughter a "Rosebud."

MY EXPERIENCE AS A SECRETARY IN THE PENTAGON, WORLD WAR II

by
Mabel Wolford Myrick

Kimberly, Alabama

Mabel Wolford in front of the U. S. Capitol in Washington, D. C. in 1944

Just before I finished Mortimer Jordan High School in Morris, Alabama in 1944, a representative from the government visited our school, giving the typing/shorthand graduates a chance to be tested for possible employment in Washington, D. C. A number from our class took the test and about seven signed up to go. The morning we were to take the train to Washington, only two of us showed up.

Upon arrival in D. C., I was assigned to the War Department in the Pentagon building. My friend was assigned to the Navy Department. My first job was in the Procedures Section. My superior was Major Joseph Downs. I took dictation not only from Major Downs, but also from about a dozen others in our section. My duties included correspondence, maintaining contact with personnel of our office in travel status, filing reports, and answering the telephone.

I had four brothers in service. I was able to see three of them while I was in D. C., but could never get any two of them together at the same time. After I was there about six months, one of my brothers was killed in France and my parents wanted me to return home. I was transferred to Birmingham Ordnance. After six months, I was contacted by Major Downs regarding the possibility of returning to the Pentagon. I went back, and was assigned to the Air Force, filing reports of secret bombing missions in ETO.

As soon as an opening occurred in the Procedures Section, I was transferred back. My new boss was Colonel Earl H. Study, who dictated letters for the signature of Secretary of War, Henry L. Stimson. Since we had to have 13 copies, I had to type it several times, using a manual typewriter and carbon paper. Then I would be sent to Mr. Stimson's office with the letters in a folder, to wait for his signature.

When the war was over, Col. Study transferred to Veterans Administration, which was located across Lafayette Park from the White House. Within a few weeks, he had me transferred to the V. A.

During my time at the V. A., I applied for and was selected to represent Alabama at a garden party to honor disabled veterans on the South Lawn at the White House. There were 823 former service men and women, and 740 officials. The most important people I met there were the disabled service men and women themselves. In the receiving line, I had the honor of shaking hands with President and Mrs. Harry Truman, Secretary of State George C. Marshall, Chief of Staff and Mrs. Dwight D. Eisenhower, Admiral of the Fleet and Mrs. Chester Nimitz, and most of the Cabinet members and their wives.

There were a lot of things to do in D. C. I made many new friends. I saw quite a few theatrical productions, went canoeing on the Potomac with my brother, and went to church at New York Avenue Presbyterian Church, which was pastored by Dr. Peter Marshall.

MARIAN THE MACHINIST
by Marian Fox
Yacolt, Washington

 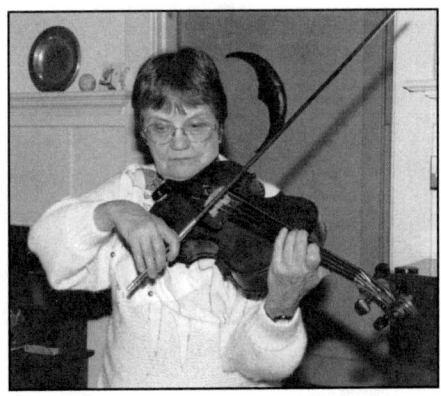

Marian Fox at age 18 (left), and in 1999 as a member of the Washington Symphony in Vancouver, Washington.

I was not Rosie the Riveter, but I was Marian the Machinist in 1942-43 in the Oregon Shipyards. War was raging in Europe. I was newly graduated from high school with no money for college and yearning to go.

My father encouraged me to apply at the shipyards. He was a lead man machinist on the night shift and had a connection or two. On the first night of work, which began at 1:00 a.m., my dad and I carried our lunch pails to the bus stop and boarded a bus filled with scruffy-looking, hard-hatted workers. There was an eerie quality in the dark quiet of the night. Most of the passengers were dozing.

We were unloaded near the entrance of the shipyards. The shipyard was immense with many Liberty ships, which carried cargo for the war, in different stages of construction. My dad took me to the machinists' shack, where I was assigned my crew and given a hard hat. Then we walked the catwalks, and climbed down the several deck ladders into the bowels of the ship called the engine room.

I met my crew, all men except for one other 18-year-old named Sharon. There I was, a scared, innocent, young girl with not the slightest idea as to what was expected.

I was sent off first thing to the tool shop in the yard off the ship. Amazingly, I did find it, and I dutifully asked for a left-handed wrench. Of course, it was the usual prank imposed on the beginner, since there is no such thing.

I did learn to help as I was asked in a variety of ways, getting tools and helping to fit parts. I adjusted quickly to sleeping days, working nights. I found out that men can be very decent to young girls, even protective.

In a few months I joined Sharon on a specific crew as a helper, then journeyman machinist, where we put up stanchions, an upright support, and hand rails on the cat walks of the various levels of the engine room. I learned to drill through the stanchion and handrail, pound in a metal pin, saw it off on either side, then file smooth. I enjoyed the job, and Sharon and I became close friends. Occasionally, the lights would go off and Sharon and I were two young women in total darkness in the guts of a ship. We would huddle together until the lights came on.

Sometimes the crew had nothing to do. Once, many metal lunch boxes were found welded down to the bunk at lunch in our tool shed. That was considered a great joke.

I worked in the yards for 10 months. The money was so good that I went to college for two years without working. There were many women working in the yards in those days – Wendy the Welder, Rosie the Riveter, and Marian the Machinist. When the men came home, most of the women returned to being homemakers. The returning men needed the jobs. I went on to become Marian the Musician.

ROSIE THE RIVETER
by Odean Gregg Blume
Aurora, Colorado

Odean Gregg Blume, Army Special Services, Tulsa, Oklahoma Recruiting and Induction Center in 1942 (left) and at age 84, retired after 30 years with Denver Public Schools

Rosie the Riveter was to women what Uncle Sam was to men during WW II. She wasn't a pin-up girl, but her image on posters was just as powerful: a bandana wrapped around her head, muscular arms, and a blue work shirt. She was the symbol of women's ability and willingness to do their part when America's able-bodied men were shipped overseas to fight during WW II.

Millions of real-life women would become Rosies before the end of the war. Women went to work in military plants, manufacturing plants, train yards, refineries, offices, and small stores around the nation. On December 1, 1944, I became a Rosie when I went to work for the Douglas Aircraft Company in Tulsa, Oklahoma. My husband was overseas. I had just completed my enlistment as an Army recruiter and went to work at Douglas for 80 cents an hour.

I could hardly believe how large the bombers were when I saw the assembly line. My legs shook with fear as I climbed the many steps to the top of the wing section where my station was located. It was there that I met a man named Fred who would be my work partner.

Fred was a very small man, probably in his fifties, but he looked more like 70. He couldn't have weighed more than 100 pounds. Fred told me that he was the rivet shooter and I was to be the "bucker." He then handed me a round, shiny, smooth piece of steel called a bucking bar. I was to hold this bar against the rivet as Fred drove it through the wing section with an air gun. The rivet had to be perfectly installed. One bad rivet could cause a fatal accident.

The first few rivets were anything but perfect. He had to drill them out and start all over again. This happened several times, but I finally got the swing of it. The size of rivets determined whether a man or a woman would work on a particular job, and the rivets we were using were very large. Fred looked at me and said, "This is a man's job, and you can refuse to do it." I was 25 years old and weighed 140 pounds. I replied, "Fred, if you can do this, so can I."

Fred and I worked together until 1945, when an announcement over the plant loud speaker informed us that Japan had surrendered. Everyone turned in their tools and marched out of the plant with a deep satisfaction that we had helped win the war. I only saw Fred one more time after the plant closed. He was walking the streets selling Watkins products. The plant was never again used to make military aircraft, even though a civilian aircraft company reopened it later.

When all of the Rosies stepped aside at the end of the war, they did it with their chins held high. Rosie was the beginning of working women in the U.S., not the end.

WORLD WAR II: THE STORY OF NORA WILLIS

by
*Nora Petrie
Nichols Willis*

Springfield, Oregon

Nora Willis, sandblasted steel spot welder, 1941-1945

In December, 1941, I was living in Marysville, Missouri, as a housewife when my husband came home and told me he was going to Kansas City to go to sheet metal school. We packed up our things and headed to Kansas City. We were both from Kansas originally, and this put us closer to home.

After he finished his sheet metal training we went to Baltimore, Maryland, to the Glenn L. Martin Plant. He went to work right away; I went to Aircraft Riveting Assembly School. After 164 hours of training, I got my certification and went to the same Glenn L. Martin Plant. I was offered a job in the office. This was funny to me, since I had worked in the fields on a farm since I was ten years old. They seemed to think that I was a school teacher and would do well in the office. I said no to that job. I told them about my training and they then offered me work as an aluminum spot welder. I worked there for a week or so, when a foreman asked for someone to go to the sandblasted steel department as a sandblasted steel spot welder. I volunteered and became the only woman in the department.

The first thing the foreman told me to do was to go and check out a bucket of spots. I asked him to go and get them for me while I was setting up my tools (I knew he was kidding). His name was Lou Exter. He laughed and said, "I usually get the new people on that one."

I became very close friends with many of the ladies that worked in this plant. We kept in touch for a time, but eventually I lost track of them.

While in Baltimore, Maryland at Glenn L. Martin plant in Sparrow Point, I worked on the *Mars*. It was a cargo seaplane, and one of the largest planes built at that time. When we finished the first plane, the plant had a picnic to acknowledge it.

I remember a day when we were about halfway through our shift. A plane was ready to go out of the building. It was fully armed, when suddenly all of the shells starting going off. One woman had the heels shot off her shoes. They moved us out of the area and sent us home until things could be cleaned up and it was determined safe.

I had a nickname, "Judy," because I always imitated Judy Canova. I would sing and act like her while working.

My husband and I worked there until Glenn L. Martin built a plant in Omaha, Nebraska. My husband was transferred, but they wanted me to stay in Baltimore. I quit and went with my husband to Nebraska. I applied at the Glenn L. Martin plant in Omaha and received 25 cents an hour more.

My husband joined the service in 1943, then went overseas. I moved back to Kansas and started working for North American as a sandblasted steel spot welder. I took 3 months off to have a baby, then went back to work until 1945. It was a time of my life that I don't want to forget.

WOMEN AT WORK IN DETROIT DEFENSE PLANTS

by Patricia Zublin
Daughter of Anna Maslonka Konieczny
Detroit, Michigan

Anna Ursula Maslonka Konieczny in 1942 (left) and in 1971

For many years, Anna Ursula Maslonka Konieczny, my mother, was wife, mother of two, and housekeeper to her own family. Also, she was big sister to her nine younger siblings after their mother died. When WW II started, her husband had just gone into business for himself as an independent pharmacist. We were coming out of the Depression and money was scarce. Anna saw other women going into the defense plants to replace the men who were going off to war. Friends and relatives encouraged Anna to join them.

Behind our home and across the parking lot was the Chrysler Lynch Road Plant. Parts for the Norden Bombsite were produced there, though lips were sealed until the end of the war. Down the road was the Dodge Forge Plant. Further down the road was the Plymouth Plant. It produced many vehicles used by all branches of the service. At the end of our street, there were rows and rows of Army vehicles waiting for shipment to the war zones. This row of factories produced many wheels of victory from 1942 to 1945.

Anna was hired to work in the tool crib at the Plymouth Plant because she had "a very legible handwriting," said the Personnel Director. From that day on, Anna etched ID nuers on tools and distributed them to the workers daily.

Anna joined the union, but when the war came, the union and its rules of work were put aside for the war effort. Many worked swing shifts like Anna's sister: work eight hours on the line then go home and sleep for eight hours, get up and go back to do another eight hours, etc.

Perfect attendance was a goal for Anna, and she never missed work in those years. She taught us children to be independent and reliable while she worked. Things had to be done by us because Mother was helping our country to win the war. We learned to buy groceries with ration books, and not waste scarce items of sugar, butter, and meat. Dad had a ration book for gas, which he used for trips related to his pharmacy. Most travel was by public transportation.

Anna was a role model for me and for many of the females in her circle of friends and relatives. She was a devout Christian, with prayer and faith very central to her existence. She was a tireless worker. She was interpreter and translator of legal papers for her Polish neighbors. She read letters from Poland to neighbors who were worrying about those they left behind in the war torn "old country."

When the war ended and the young men began coming home, Anna's philosophy was that the returning veterans needed their jobs back to support themselves and their families. She quit working at the defense plant in 1945 and went to work as a clerk for her husband in his pharmacy. Anna worked with him until the very day she died at the age of 71 in 1973.

MY PARACHUTE STORY: A PACKER AND GOVERNMENT INSPECTOR

by
Lola M. Bates Putnam

Charlotte, North Carolina

Lola May Bates Putnam in her Inspector's uniform in the 1940's

When WW II broke out and I needed to keep busy, I applied for a government job advertised in the local paper. I went to work, rather into training, in Oakland, California. I learned all about covering airplane wings with canvas, all about industrial sewing machines, how to handle a tool shop, and various other things, but most of all, I learned the how! what! and when! of a parachute, which I loved to handle. I had a great instructor. I'm sorry I've let his name slip, as I'm 85 and I can't keep all names in my mind.

After three months, we were transferred to McClend Field at Sacramento, California, where I trained for several months. The instructors were great and I enjoyed my work. There were around 150 women on this project. They all worked hard, and we had to learn every process printed in a book, which I kept for years. I studied hard and had a roommate who made me learn, so after some time, we were all checked out as parachute packers. That was a day I was really happy. I could unknot a chute in five minutes and I always came with an "A" in tests we took. I loved my work.

About two months after that, I was called into the trainer's office, which was an unusual thing, so I sweated till the time came. There were three overseers, or supervisors, there, so you can imagine how I felt. I just knew that I was going to get my walking papers or some usual thing, but they were all smiles and were really nice to me. They said, "You have been selected to be a Government Parachute Inspector, as we know that you will be a good one."

I spoke up and said that there were people there that were better than me. They spoke up, saying I was their best out of 150 girls, so I accepted the responsibility graciously, till they said they wanted me to pick eight qualified girls to work under me. At that time, I said, "No, I can't do that." I broke down and cried, I remember.

They said, "You have to; you are the only one." So with some persuasion, I accepted the position. I hated to make any girl feel bad if I didn't choose her. All of the girls were around me trying to be selected, but I picked the best ones and those who would cooperate with one another. We did a good job. We had to watch all the packers quite closely and box the chutes. I had to stamp them out and send them on to their destinations. Some officers came in to meet the packers, and they had jumped in the chutes they had packed. That was so exciting for the girls.

One girl left a chute bag in a chute. When I lifted the pack, I knew it was too heavy, so I made the packer open the chute. She was pretty upset, but had to be reported to my supervisors. She was watched closely from then on.

I finally transferred to Alameda Air Field, Alameda, California, where I inspected the airplane instruments and the rivets in the airplanes, mostly B-49's and big planes and parachutes.

STEEL FOR WARSHIPS
by Louise Hessek Dalzell
Huntsville, Alabama

*Louise H. Dalzell in 1942
in Pittsburgh, Pennsylvania*

I was working in Washington, D. C. for the U. S. Engineers (now the Corps of Engineers) when the terrible event of Pearl Harbor happened.

My home was originally Pittsburgh, Pennsylvania. My dear mother was a widow, having raised a family of seven children in Depression days. Four brothers were living with Mom at the time of Pearl Harbor. The four brothers went into the service, leaving Mother alone.

It was decided that I should return to Pittsburgh to be with Mom, as it was a difficult time for her with two boys in the Army and two in the Navy.

I secured employment in the Industrial Engineering

Department city office in Pittsburgh at Carnegie-Illinois Steel (U. S. Steel).

Many plants were losing to the war young men who were working as industrial engineers. To my surprise, I was selected to attend an accelerated Industrial Engineering course at the University of Pittsburgh. Other women were selected from the plants. Upon completion, I was assigned to the Homestead plant. I was delighted to have the assignment and the opportunity to open a new field for women.

The work involved time and motion studies, methods, job evaluation, production planning, etc., working in different parts of the plant. It was most interesting and a challenge, and I am grateful to have had the opportunity.

We were not very popular with the employees in the steel plant. They thought of us as "efficiency experts" who were finding ways for them to lose their jobs.

We did our jobs to simplify work and find ways to increase production. Still, we were greeted with, "Here they come again..."

I worked from 1942-1944.

Louise in 2004, Huntsville, Alabama

I BUILT AIRPLANES SO THE BOYS COULD WIN THE WAR

by Dr. Madalynne King Norick
Oklahoma City, Oklahoma

Madalynne Norick with her son, Ronald James, on his third birthday on August 5, 1944 (left), and in 2004.

My defense work started when my husband Jim, a Navy Storekeeper, went aboard ship for duty in the south Pacific. At the time, our son, Ron, was two years old. A friend of mine, who was also an artist, decided we should help on the home front, so we applied for a job at the Douglas plant that was being built in Oklahoma City.

We had grand ideas of having a studio for artistic work, but a surprise awaited us. A train track ran through the west side of the mile-long building where heavy equipment, was unloaded, including drop-hammers and all the necessary tools it took to build a C-47 airplane. Men would hammer in U. S. numbers on the various pieces of equipment, and our "artistic" job was to take a bucket of yellow paint and with a wide brush, paint the numbers and wipe off the excess with a cloth.

Because of our job, we had bicycles and badges that would allow us to go anywhere in the plant. All others had to stay in their departments. At this time, the plant was about half completed, with the #1 plane screened off. With our badges, we got inside and looked all over the plane and nobody bothered us.

Later, I reluctantly gave up my bicycle and Go badge and took a job in the Executive Lobby, dispatching a courier service to the airport to pick up persons who purchased the planes. I vividly remember seeing the Russians and the big red star on the planes on the runway getting ready to leave. Later, I found out the *Enola Gay* was modified here at the Oklahoma City plant.

In order to spend more time with our son, Ron, I got a job on the swing shift, answering trouble calls and sending emergency personnel to fix the problems. One night, when things were quiet, my supervisor and I were visiting, and all of a sudden, I fainted and fell in his lap. When I awakened, I was lying on the conference table with eight supervisors staring at me. I started crying and just knew something had happened to my husband. Sure enough, later in a V-Mail from Jim, I found out he had shot down a twin-engine Betty Kamikaze plane during the invasion of Leyte Gulf in the Philippines.

When the announcement came over the loudspeaker at the Douglas plant that the war was over and people could leave early, I cried and finished my shift, then awaited word when Jim would come home.

I will always remember my working at the Douglas Aircraft Plant, which is now Tinker Air Force Maintenance Base, and in a small way, doing my part to get my husband and all the other men home.

LELA'S "ROSIE" UNIFORM

by
Lela Morlan McDaniel

Salem, Virginia

Lela Morlan McDaniel in 1945 (inset) and in her Rosie uniform in 2004

I grew up in Missouri in a large family. During the period of 1941-45, I took training at Poplar Bluff, Missouri through NYA in machine shop. I worked at Curtiss Wright (now McDonnell Douglas) at Lambert Airport and wore the uniform seen pictured above. There I ran milling machines, screw machines, and the drill press, and made airplane parts. I also took blueprint reading classes a couple of hours a week.

Times were very difficult and housing and transportation were scarce. Many times I have ridden a bus to the end of the line and walked 19 blocks at 3:00 a.m. in the morning just to get home to get a few hours sleep before starting over again. Most working shifts were 10 to 12 hours long, six to seven days a week.

Our family (two brothers, ages 13 and 15, one sister, age 10, and my father) moved to Portland, Oregon. We rode a train for four days that was so crowded with soldiers that we had to stand up or sit in the floor. In 1945, I went to work at Washore Turkey Association, providing meat and eggs that were shipped to be dried for the Army. My job included standing between a Sergeant and a Lieutenant from the Army who inspected the entrails of the turkey after I eviscerated it. I also worked in the turkey hatchery, where one of the unique skills I learned was to determine the gender of the turkey polts.

Recreation during the war included going to Forest Park, the zoo, or meeting my four friends and going skating at the all-night skating rink after we got off work at 1:00 a.m. We also enjoyed listening to the opera music at Forest Park (we couldn't go in because the tickets were too expensive). I continue to have contact with two of those friends. Due to the return of soldiers to their jobs, I was laid off and went to work at Carter Carburetor, also in St. Louis, where I operated a "swedger" and a screw machine.

My oldest sister, Marguerite, saved the uniform after the war and it was returned to me after her death in March, 1999. Although I learned a lot during that time, I was happy and sad, for nearly every day we heard of the death of someone we knew.

I met and married a Navy guy in 1946 and moved to Virginia. I have been a widow since 1990 and am retired from the VA Canteen Services. We had two children and two grandchildren, and now I have six great-grandchildren and continue to live in Salem, Virginia.

TRUE LOVE STILL EXISTS
by Ruth Slack Sedwick
Birmingham, Alabama

When this picture was taken of Ruth Slack in 1940
in Columbus, Ohio, she gave an 8 x 10 copy to
her friend, who became her husband!

On Sunday, December 7, 1941, I was visiting my parents on the farm in central Ohio, when news came over the radio that Japanese fighter planes had bombed Pearl Harbor, Hawaii.

I had a secretarial job with a finance company in Columbus, and my friend worked for a coal mining machinery factory. Factories began changing to wartime facilities. And there was rationing of many things. I decided to apply to Curtiss Wright Airplane Plant.

I was hired for the steno pool. It turned out to be very boring, so I asked my supervisor for a better job. Within a week, I was offered a most challenging job – to be secretary in the office of General Claire Chenault (who spent most of his time in China). He returned to Curtiss Wright periodically to inspect the progress. I loved the job!

In the meantime, my friend received a notice from Uncle Sam, saying, "I Want You." He preferred not to be in the Army, so he enlisted in the Navy Seabees. He left town for training in March, 1942, and served one year in the Aleutian Islands before returning for a 30-day leave. Just before shipping out to the Aleutians, he had a weekend pass to come home. He telephoned me and said, "Go to the court house and get the marriage license and meet the train Friday afternoon." At the court house, they just laughed at me. For one thing, I was not of legal age, and a three-day waiting period was law.

When he arrived on Friday, I told him the bad news. He said, "Don't worry, my sister and her husband went to Kentucky; they will go with us." They did!

My husband left Sunday morning and went back to camp. I went back to work. It was a year before I saw him again, when he returned for a thirty-day leave. Afterwards, he went to the west coast to be shipped out to Guam and Okinawa. I spent many volunteer hours rolling bandages for the American Red Cross.

We celebrated our 62nd wedding anniversary on May 30, 2004.

Gib and Ruth Sedwick, as featured in The Birmingham News *in 2003 for participating in the Black and White Ball as supporters of Shepherd Center-Southside.*

THE FAMILY ROSE GARDEN
by Patricia Tringe van Betten
Blue Diamond, Nevada

 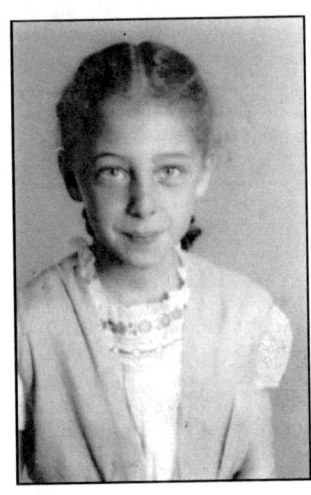

Mary Tringe (left) in her Victory Garden in the 1940's. On the right is Mary's daughter, Patricia, in third grade.

Although I first thought I was the first Rosie in our family, I can't tell you how delighted I am to defer to my 90-year-old mother and become her Rosebud in ARRA.

I first met Fran Carter, ARRA Executive Director, when we were both serving as delegates to the National Silver Haired Congress in Washington, D. C. As she was explaining the new ARRA organization to me, I said, "Oh, Fran, I believe I may qualify as a volunteer!" I proudly explained that, in the 1940's, our third grade class at Greeneville Grade School in Norwich, Connecticut, learned to knit so that we could knit small woolen squares. The squares were then sent off to be stitched together to make an afghan for a soldier. We felt quite important. (As I look back, I can only imagine what those squares looked like!! But they were filled with love, no doubt about it.) Fran said I definitely qualified to be a Rosie. My daughter, Melanie van Betten Jeffcoat, and my granddaughters, Hannah and Chloe, are Rosebuds.

Like many of my grade school classmates, I felt very connected to the war effort. Two of my uncles served in the Navy, one served in the Army, and another served in the Coast Guard. As I was talking about the Rosie memory with my 90-year-old mother, she said, "Oh, I did that, too. I walked with my girlfriends to that white church on the corner in Norwichtown, once a week. The Red Cross was there with yarn and knitting needles. We would knit squares for people to put together to make blankets for the soldiers." There we were, a generation apart, working on the same effort. I was thrilled to learn about it!

"Oh, Mom," I said, "YOU are the Rosie! And I am happy to know that we are your Rosebuds!" What a wonderful discovery. So here we are, four generations strong, one Rosie and four Rosebuds. The Rosie in our family is Mary Cellucci Tringe, born September 8, 1913.

My father, William Tringe, tried to join the Navy. He was enthusiastic as he and my mom drove to Providence, Rhode Island to enlist, but he was turned down, perhaps because he had three small children. He returned to his job at the American Thermos Bottle Company in Norwich, where he was a glass blower. But his civilian job was vital to the war effort. Research shows that the American Thermos Bottle Company, particularly the glassblowers, played an important role, as more than 98% of the company's output during that time was for military use and atomic energy laboratories.

Pat, Mary, Melanie, Chloe, and Hannah in 2004

ROSIE TIMES TWO

by
Marie Reichert Beard

Baltimore, Maryland

Marie Reichert Beard (left) and Catherine Reichert, a "sister riveting team" in the 1940's

When I turned 18 years old in 1942, it was common knowledge that women were being hired to work at Glenn L. Martin Aircraft in Baltimore, Maryland. My older sister and I decided that this opportunity to help in the war effort and to help our farming family was the right decision for us. We were ready to trade in our hoes.

We applied for production jobs at Martin's Aircraft and were immediately employed. I wore my first pair of trousers and was away from home 12 hours a day! I was outfitted with a toolbox and riveting tools for my job. After training, we became "the champion sister riveting team."

We particularly constructed a section of the wing on the PBM-3 Land and Sea aircraft. Catherine riveted and I bucked, then we would change positions. Seven days a week we caught the bus that stopped at the end of our lane and took us to Middle River, ten miles away. Arriving home at dinnertime, we could still help with canning vegetables and doing homestead chores. We were so impressed with earning 60 cents an hour, but we soon discovered that there was no time and very few products to spend our money on. Our savings accounts grew, after helping with our parents' needs.

Not only did working at Martin's during the war build my self-esteem and prepare me for the workplace the rest of my life, it was also where I met my husband-to-be. Early in the war, he was a sheet metal fitter at the plant, until he was drafted to serve in the occupation of Japan. At the conclusion of the war, our sister team was frequently laid off, as the men returned to industry. My career officially ended at Martin's soon after my marriage in 1949, with news that I was expecting a baby. Pregnant women were not allowed to work in production, as there were now men to replace us.

At the time, I had no idea that I was taking a place in history, but I look back with pride at the role I played during WW II, and I appreciate this opportunity to tell my story.

Marie, shown here in 2004, volunteers at a community hospital, sewing pillows for breast surgery and cardiac patients. She enjoys family, friends, and traveling.

HAVE RIVET GUN, WILL TRAVEL
by Dena Mai Peach Berry
Crescent City, California

Dena Mai Peach Berry (left) and with fellow "cigarette girls" as they were known when they traveled with the Camel Caravan, a variety show for the armed forces.

After 15 weeks of intense training at Anderson Airplane School in Nashville, Tennessee, Uncle Sam bought first-class train tickets for 20 young aircraft sheet metal mechanics – all girls – and shipped them off to work at Buckingham Air Force Base (a gunnery school) near Ft. Myers, Florida. Our main job was to patch up holes the gunners shot through the fuselage when they lost control of the gun turret.

The first day on the job, we witnessed a B-26 explode on landing, killing all aboard. Another day, while working on the line, I watched a worker being decapitated by the propeller of a moving plane. During a thunder storm, when all ships had been called in, we watched in horror as one pilot flew his ship directly into a thunder cloud and burst into splinters, even while the tower was screaming directions for his approach to the landing strip.

We also repaired planes assigned to Page Field, where fighter pilots were trained. Officers stationed at Page Field were quartered at the Royal Palms Hotel in Ft. Myers, a beautiful old hotel on a huge acreage, with a glassed-in dining room, cocktail lounge and ballroom, and a massive swimming pool. Since we girls were civil service employees, we were allowed to live there, and six of us decided to do so. With two of us to a room at $35 a month with daily maid service and a morning wake-up call, we felt like we were on vacation.

We worked long hours six days a week, and it was a thrill to come home to this beautiful hotel and see all those handsome Lieutenants on the veranda waiting for us to start the evening. Usually we had to ration our time: one date for cocktails and dinner, another for dancing, and finally another for a moonlight swim. Unfortunately, Florida had a midnight curfew, and that meant everybody out of the pool at 12:00 sharp. The desk clerk was an old fuddy-duddy who liked to play tricks with the pool lights – lights off, lights on. It was a panic to watch the bodies fall out over the sides of the pool when the lights flashed on, with the desk clerk frantically running out to catch somebody. That was our favorite game. One night someone threw him into the pool, clothes and all, and he almost drowned.

Page Field lost a lot of pilots during their short six-week training course. They bailed out of falling ships, and their parachutes were caught in the tail section, or they went down with the ship. The pick-up line in those days was the same old sad story: "This might be my last day on earth, and I'm going to have all the fun I can." In too many cases, this turned out to be true.

I worked on the home front from August 1941 to September 1945. This is one story of many, some with gun, some without.

MY STORY AS ROSIE THE RIVETER
by Fannie Eleanor Watson Shaffer
Los Banos, California

Fannie Shaffer with her husband in the 1940's (left) and more recently

Many years have traveled by now, and I am glad I am still here to tell my story. I graduated from high school in 1943 and found us (the U. S.) in the middle of WW II, both in the eastern and western sectors of the world. The men of our class were being drafted into the service like flies, and many of the girls were also doing their part in the war efforts. Due to illness, I didn't join them until August, 1943.

Since I was not quite 18 years of age, a work permit was required to do factory work. I left my home town, a small town in Ohio, and took a sleeping room in Canton, Ohio where I began working in an aircraft factory (Berger Aircraft). The factory made mostly wings for B-32 bombers. I was taught how to make the hinges for the wing flaps.

Safety was of great importance in our shop. The ladies were to wear hair nets and/or scarves tied in a triangle to cover all the hair. Also, steel-toed shoes were mandatory.

The plant was not air conditioned and it was very hot in the summer time. Salt tablet dispensers were placed near the water fountains throughout the plant. Upon arriving to work we would pick up our time cards at the window and punch them into a time clock. They didn't seem to fire people back then if they were 15 minutes late but they would dock them one hour of pay for anything over 15 minutes.

There was a large lunchroom. Nearly every female used to smoke in that lunchroom. I never had smoked before. One day I bought a pack from the cigarette machine and after lunch I lit one up with the rest of the ladies. I took one puff and I felt so guilty and ashamed that I held the rest of the cigarette under the table until it burned my fingers.

The women worked two shifts, daylight and afternoon. Canton, being a large city, had a City Square where all the buses from the outer parts of town came. The bus service found that the regular buses were too small to hold all the employees going to the plant, so they employed some cattle-cars which ran only to and from the City Square. The plant where I worked was outside the city limits. There was a small restaurant where we got off the bus, and they served incredible Coney Island hot dogs. The juke box played the Ink Spots singing "If I Didn't Care" and "Paper Doll," the Andrews Sisters singing "Don't Sit Under the Apple Tree with Anyone Else But Me," and many other favorites.

I was introduced to my late husband in October, 1943. He had been examined for induction to the service but was so thin they sent him home for another nine months. He worked until his second exam, when he was inducted into the Navy in April, 1944. I continued to work as "Rosie" until February, 1945. My sweetheart returned home on leave in March, 1945 and we were married. He returned from the Navy after the war in January, 1946. We had four children and moved to California, living very happily for 53 years until our marriage ended June 23, 1998, when my sweetheart passed away from ALS.

FROM FARM GIRL TO FACTORY WORKER
by Mary J. Maslonka Du Lac
Harper Woods, Michigan

Mary Maslonka Du Lac in the 1940's

I grew up on a farm near Metz, Michigan, and farming was a hard way of life. At age 18, I left home and took a low-paying job housekeeping in Alpena, Michigan. After three years, I decided to follow my older siblings to Detroit for better wages working in the automobile factories. Little did I know what the future had in store for me.

In 1936, at the age of 21, I arrived in Detroit and lived with my sisters while looking for work. By 1937, I had found employment at Jenks and Muir Company, an automobile spring manufacturer.

On February 3, 1940, Donald Du Lac, a Great Lakes sailor, and I were married. I became a stay-at-home housewife. In 1941, WW II began and life became very different for us. By 1942, my husband joined the U. S. Navy. He left to serve in the Pacific Theater of Operations, just before our only child, Bernard, was born in February of 1943. My husband did not hold his son until 1945!

With assistance from my sisters and their families, who helped care for our son, I went back to work in the factory. The Jenks and Muir Company was now owned by Murray Body, another automobile parts manufacturer. I was transferred to the new company that had converted from automobile work to fabricating parts for the B-17 bombers. I became a part of the war effort.

Although I trained for several jobs that spanned from 1942 to 1945, I mostly operated a riveting machine that secured metal outer skins to the inner ribs or supports of the plane. I also used a riveting gun to secure the outer nose cone section of the aircraft. Sometimes I worked as a "bucker." A bucker was a person who worked inside the nose cone holding a large square steel bar about a foot long against the tail end of the rivets, while a fellow riveter impacted the rivets to secure the metal sheets to the air frame assembly.

We worked ten-hour days, sometimes seven days a week, for the next three years. I worked hard and gave them the very best I could! When I went home each night feeling very tired, I would always take time to kneel down and pray to God to end the war and bring my husband and all our boys safely home.

Now I am 89 years old and a widow, a grandmother and great-grandmother. I have survived cancer three times. I am almost deaf from nerve damage to my ears caused by the long hours of noise from riveting without ear protection. My memories of those days in the factory are filled with many places and faces from that period of time when we exhibited extraordinary physical and mental strength as the working women of World War II. I was Rosie the Riveter!

A DAY IN THE LIFE OF A ROSIE THE RIVETER DURING WW II

by
Mildred "Millie" Crow Sargent

Nashville, Tennessee

*Millie Crow Sargent
in 1944*

At 5:00 a.m., the alarm clock went off in the back bedroom of the house where all of my husband's family lived, eight adults and two children, in Highland Park, Michigan. The adults were all war workers. My husband and his brothers, Stanley and Basil, worked at Detroit Tap and Tool, as precision grinders on aircraft instruments. My father-in-law, Harden Crow, and his wife, Hallie, worked at Plymouth Motor Company, on trucks, tanks, and parachutes. Basil's wife, Louise, worked there, also. Stanley's wife, Gracie, worked at Woodall Industries with me. She tested metals for strength. I was the only riveter. Hallie arose at the sound of the alarm and hurried through our bedroom to the bathroom to get ready for the daytime shift at Plymouth.

I had gotten to bed about 2:00 a.m. The noise did not usually wake me, but it woke my two-year-old son, Larry, who was sleeping in a crib in the room. This was a problem for me, because everyone else in the house was sleeping for an afternoon or midnight shift. I dragged myself from bed, put a clean diaper on him, and fed him. However, he wanted to play. I surely didn't, after only about three hours of sleep, but I had to stay up with him.

Gracie and I prepared dinner for the three brothers. They would, in turn, clear away the dishes and watch after Larry. I would dress in my uniform, a navy blue twill long-sleeved shirt (to protect against aluminum drill shavings), and matching slacks. I had been told that "nice" girls did not wear slacks, but I soon learned at the plant that they were best for safety, as well as modesty's sake.

After my arrival at Woodall Industries, I punched the time clock and donned my apron, which had several pockets for different size rivets and pins for holding the aluminum skins onto the metal frames. The skins were dimpled to fit into counter-sunk holes in the frame. We used some of the rivets to tie the cast aluminum oil pan to the Speed Ring that covered the motor of the Curtiss-Wright "Hell Diver." It was a carrier-based plane, used mostly in the Pacific.

I was on the outside of the ring, but my partner, Ethel Klepian, was on the inside. She used a metal bucking bar for smashing down the bucktail of the rivet. There was a great deal of pride when we finished a speed ring and removed it from the jig. We knew that we had completed part of a plane that would save a soldier's life.

At the end of the shift, we returned home to repeat the same routine. I often wonder how I worked so many times with so little sleep. However, I was young and foolish, and I could function for a time. I enjoyed my work, and I felt a patriotic urge to keep going, or I couldn't have made it.

In the last year of the war, I pulled the ligaments in my right thumb while bowling, and I had to move to time-keeping. I was able to get an apartment in a government housing unit near the plant. It had a nursery for my son, and it was close enough to walk to work. I was transferred to the day shift, and life was then much easier.

HIGH SCHOOL AND WAR-TIME MEMORIES
by Eileen Trout Blackler
Sun City, Arizona

Eileen Blackler in 1944, graduating from Oregon City High School

World War II started during my freshman year of high school at Girls' Polytechnic in Portland, Oregon. I still remember when they called an assembly on Monday, December 8, and we listened to President Roosevelt declare war, via radio. It was a sober time and I still have goose-bumps when I remember. We all stood up at the playing of our National Anthem, feeling in a state of shock! It was an experience for me to see the Japanese girls (classmates) around me who did *not* stand. I realize now how bewildered they must have felt!

But, as we know, life must go on, and, as the war progressed, we all did what we could on the home front. So many of the boys went off to war and I found myself writing letters. I wrote to 32 boys on a regular basis—and when I became engaged at the tender age of 16, I wrote to *him* every day, too – for three years!

It's hard to recall all the life changes that occur, growing up during war time, but it was a busy time! I remember going to the USO a lot, and how we would often bring three and four boys home on the bus for dinner on Sundays and special times of the year.

One night a week, at least, I volunteered to work at the Albetina Kerr Children's Home in the Lane Ward. There were between 20 and 30 babies, all under six months old. We changed many diapers and held, rocked, and bottle-fed all evening.

When I was old enough to get a work permit, during summertime when school was out, I worked in the Air Base fountain at the commissary. There we made the best, richest, thickest milkshakes, and real ice cream sodas for "the boys" and tried to make light talk as they were getting prepared to go "over there."

Finally in 1944, I graduated high school. Then I took a job at Commercial Iron Works (ship yard). I wasn't a riveter, guess I was too young. I worked in the typing pool, doing mostly copy work. It was quite a thrill to go down and see the ships when they were commissioned and sent out to active duty. It made us feel like we were doing something for the war effort.

Eileen in 2004

Through the years I have seen a lot of results of war and hate, and I pray often that somehow our nation can manage to promote peace and love for one another – in the whole world!

WANDA THE WELDER
by Helen M. Turner
Lacey, Washington

Helen Turner in 1942 at age 17 (left), and with two tiny friends in 2004

In 1941, I was a high school senior in Wallace, Idaho. On December 7, our family was at the dinner table with the radio playing. The program was interrupted with the announcement that Japan had bombed Pearl Harbor and we were at war. I graduated in May, 1942, and our family moved to Portland, Oregon. My dad and I were hired as welders at two different Kaiser shipyards. I think my dad was actually a little proud that his 18-year-old daughter was doing the same work he was. (Dad served in the Army in France during WW I.) When the title "Rosie the Riveter" first appeared, Grandma dubbed me Wanda the Welder.

First came two weeks in welding school. One day, when I didn't yet have my full protective gear, only leather "chaps" that covered the front of my slacks, someone began pounding the seat of my pants. I raised my welding hood and turned to discover that it was the instructor administering the beating. Turned out, sparks from the overhead weld had caught my slacks on fire. He was trying to put out the flame, all the while ready to duck in case I slugged him for getting so fresh.

Helen in her welding gear

Although I hated the reason for our jobs (war), I loved the job itself. It was a great experience to climb around those huge hulls and see how they were put together. There were risks, of course. One day, on three hours' sleep, I went and donated blood. At work, I was welding in double bottoms, very small spaces between the bottom deck and the ship's hull. All went well until I needed to go get more welding rods. I couldn't move! Perhaps it was the loss of blood, combined with too little sleep. I had no strength. I lay there for what seemed like hours before I was finally able to pull myself out. Later, I began to notice signs of claustrophobia. Hmmm. Wonder why?

Another time I was walking on the top deck and, for some reason, turned to look where I'd just been. There was a large square opening in that deck and in each deck directly below, all the very long way to the bottom. There had been a string of warning lights and signs around the hole, but they had been knocked down. A few inches over and I'd have made a deadly descent all the way to the bottom deck. Someone must have been watching over me!

I had to walk alone ten blocks in the dark at the end of the shift. The first few nights, a pack of neighborhood dogs came running out, growling, but I managed to make friends with them and, after that, they would come running, with tails wagging, and accompany me home, quietly.

It was dirty, grimy work, but I enjoyed it—danger, dirt, dogs, and all. I never considered it a sacrifice, or in any way comparable to the effort and sacrifice of our troops.

FROM ROSIE TO RETIREMENT
by Vera M. Fox
Baltimore, Maryland

Vera M. Fox as she appeared on the job in a newspaper clipping in the 1940's

    I am proud to say I was one of the many women who worked in a defense plant during WW II. I started working at Glenn L. Martin in 1945 and remained there until I was laid off in 1962. I enjoyed my days as "Rosie the Riveter," and was proud to serve my country in any way that I could. The job I had was doing the riveting on PBM planes and the C-Master.

    There was also an added bonus to being Rosie the Riveter. I met the love of my life, as he was working there, too. In May, we will be married for 57 happy years.

    My husband was transferred to California to the Vanderburg Air Force Base for a while and then transferred to

Colorado. I worked in Colorado also until we both retired. We returned to Maryland and both began a new career at Johns Hopkins Hospital. My husband was a dietary supervisor and I worked in the Post Office until our second retirement. After our second retirement, we were able to enjoy six months of every year for 21 years in sunny Florida.

We have many memories of our tenure at the Glenn L. Martin plant. It was an honor to be part of the family at the Glenn L. Martin Plant and a privilege to help our country. We will never forget the experience. Three of my sisters also worked for the Glenn L. Martin Plant. We met many friends and still keep in touch. We try to make it to the homecoming picnic celebration every year. It is wonderful to know that Rosie the Riveter will never be forgotten.

Mr. and Mrs. C. H. Fox in Florida in 2004

THE KANSAS CONNECTION
by Jeanette Salerno
Daughter of Caroline "Carrie" Riley
Newton, Kansas

Carrie Riley in the 1940's and (right) walking home one day on Douglas Street in Wichita, Kansas

During WW II, our Rosie, Caroline "Carrie" Riley, was a riveter for G & H Manufacturing Company in Wichita, Kansas. Her job was riveting wing pieces. Completed wings were sent across town to Boeing Aircraft for final assembly.

We lived in Newton, 30 miles north of Wichita. Newton was a small railroad town on the Santa Fe main line. Mother and three of her VFW friends carpooled to Wichita to help with the war effort. They were wives of WW I soldiers. Our dad served in France with Harry S. Truman's Missouri 35th Division.

At seven years old, I was not too happy about Mother being away from home. Most every day I watched and waited for her from my post on the front lawn.

On laundry day, my sister Jerri and I would search mother's coverall pockets for stray light green or blue treasured rivets. Occasionally she would bring us Hershey bars and gum for a surprise.

Most days Rosie came home very tired as travel and work took a lot of energy, especially days when her job was bracing (bucking) rivets. The bucking process provided stability on the back side, thus securing the rivets.

Rosie also gave time to the USO. The USO was located on Main Street across from the train depot. Troop trains frequently came to town, making quick stops. As trains approached, the ladies would cross the street with trays of coffee, snacks, paper, pencils, and small packs of cigarettes for the excited troops. They were a noisy and happy group, all reaching out the windows for the meager gifts.

Everyone in town was eager to do their part, whether working in a defense plant, growing a victory garden, saving foil, or scrapping for metal.

On our block of East Ninth Street there were eight young sons called to duty. We will always remember their courage and the two houses with a gold star in the window.

After JFK's death in 1963, Newton had a parade down Main Street. Mother volunteered to carry a heavy American flag for the fallen President.

Rosies will be remembered for many generations for their contributions and sacrifices. Thank you all.

Carrie's Rosebuds: Jeanette Salerno, Diane Sutherlin, Maria Wilson, Gina Vairo, and Riley Sutherlin

MY FIRST JOB

by

Elaine Smith O'Quinn

Yulee, Florida

Elaine O'Quinn (right) in the 1940's

In May, 1943, I graduated from high school in the small town of Neal, Kansas. My class consisted of six people, which were four boys and two girls.

Right after graduation, I went to Wichita, Kansas to get a job at Boeing Aircraft Compay. I went to the employment office of Boeing, as they were hiring riveters. The person I saw was a lady, and you always saw the same person each visit. She kept telling me I was too small (five feet tall and 100 pounds). That was a bunch of crock, as size didn't make any difference in certain areas of the plane. I went every day and finally she said she was tired of seeing my face and hired me.

I went to riveting school for two weeks and then to the plant. I had a partner named Jessie and we riveted down the pilot's floor of the B-29. Jessie was 35 years old and I thought she was so old. She made a good partner and we made a great team and we got along very well. I drove the rivets and she bucked them. We worked the second shift. Sometimes a group would go roller-skating on Thursday after work at 4:00 in the morning. The rink opened up for the workers once a week.

On the weekends, we would go to one of the nightclubs to dance with the service men. There were several nightclubs and plenty of service men, as there were seven bases that were close enough to Wichita that the service men came in for the weekend.

I met my husband on one of those weekends. We dated for several months and he wanted to get married but I said I was not going to get married till the war was over. When they declared the end of the war, he came to see me and said, "Honey, the war is over!" We were married a month later and had 46½ years of a wonderful marriage. He was a Georgia boy, so that is how I became a Southerner rather than a Midwesterner.

Elaine in 2000

LOCKHEED AIRCRAFT – THAT'S WHERE I WAS
by Polly Nikolaisen
Kalispell, Montana

Polly Nikolaisen in the 1940's (left), and ringing in the New Year in 2004

A BIG COUNTRY SALUTE TO ALL THE VETERANS
Who served without knowing their fate.
World War II, I worked and remember
That Lockheed made the P-38.

Like many others from across the country, I migrated from a (Depression years) farm in North Dakota to southern California. I started working at Lockheed Aircraft for 51 cents an hour! I worked in the Sales Department in the biggest office I have ever seen, before or since. The girls working near me didn't know that I was a proud farmer – their favorite slams when they didn't like something were "dumb farmer" or "bunch of farmers." The Department Manager called me in one day and said he would like to promote me to Supervisor, but he couldn't because I was a woman.

Lockheed parking lots were camouflaged with chicken wire and feathers so cars could not be seen from the air. All windows in the area were blacked out so no light showed. I won't say we weren't afraid of being bombed after Pearl Harbor. Gas and many items were rationed, but I remember the salesman who brought me a pair of scarce nylons.

Twice we received "E" for Excellence pins from the government for completing contracts ahead of time. When I was in Norway in 1984, I shared one of my "E" pins with a relative to acknowledge to him and his family the Underground Resistance Work he did during the war when Germany invaded Norway.

Four of my brothers served their country in the Army, Navy, and Marines. I worked with sisters, wives, mothers, and sweethearts. Even those who lost their loved ones bravely showed their loyalty to our troops.

My JOY was shared at the overwhelming celebration held at Hollywood and Vine, August 14, 1945, when the victory announcement was heard. Many of us Rosies shared in the worldwide V-J celebration. California governor Earl Warren said, "It is yet to be determined if this day is to be the greatest day in all our history or just the end of another war." August, 2005 marked 60 years since that historic day. Now, again, it's prayers for PEACE.

Polly with her model P-38

MEMORIES OF "ROSIE THE RIVETER" OF WORLD WAR II

by *Carrie Hill Thomas*
Tuttle, Oklahoma

Carrie Hill Thomas in 1943, standing beside the 1938 pickup truck she drove to work as a Rosie

I, Carrie Hill Thomas, with my husband, Rullon, and our children, Joyce and Bud, lived on a farm in Newcastle, Oklahoma. I heated water for our gasoline Maytag washer; we had kerosene lamps and ice for the refrigerator. I ironed with a flat iron that had to be heated on a stove. I was a member of the Bridge Creek 4-H Club in school. Lizzie Basher and Elsie Langston taught us girls how to can food. This gift has served me well all my life.

In 1943, I and my two sisters, Pauline and Viola, became Rosies by working on C-47 airplanes. I drove our 1938 pickup with a camper that my husband built, and picked up passengers for work at Douglas Aircraft, now

Tinker Air Force Base. We were required to wear slacks and hairnets. Until then slacks were considered unladylike.

When the plane came to our center wing section, it looked like the skeleton of an enormous fish. We would join sheets of Alcoa aluminum together by shooting rivets through metal and bucking the rivet with a bucking bar (much like a sledgehammer). The girls liked for me to do this job because I was small and could get into tight places. When the rivet hit the bar it really gave me a jolt. The inspectors watched carefully for perfection before attaching to the fuselage. One day they sent me to the tool crib for a left-handed monkey wrench – boy, was the laugh on me. When we got a break, we sat on the floor in a circle to talk and rest.

The money we earned helped us get electricity, the dream of every farmer's wife in the 1940's. We built on a bathroom and back porch. Now, at 86 years of age, I will never forget the thrill of flushing a stool and taking baths without heating water for a #3 tin tub.

When the war was over, they said, "Go home, girls, and give a GI a job." We were so glad when they came home, we gladly gave the jobs to them.

I'm proud to be called "Rosie the Riveter" of World War II.

*Carrie Thomas,
86 years young*

ROSIE THE RIVETER

by
Vernelle Brown Hasty

Albertville, Alabama

Vernelle Brown in 1942

I was born on April 13, 1922, the second of six children born to John Henry and Mary Ethyl Womack Brown in Geraldine, Alabama. I graduated from high school in May of 1942. Graduation was on a Friday night and the following Sunday I hitched a ride with my Uncle Robert Womack to Birmingham.

I found and rented a room from Mrs. Avery and her two daughters, Edna and Virginia, and Mrs. Avery's small son. I soon found employment with Harless Mattress Company sewing bandoleers, a broad belt for holding ammunition. I was only employed with them for four months before leaving by train for Wichita, Kansas.

Cessna Aircraft Company hired me and immediately sent me to sheet metal school for six weeks. Afterwards, I helped build doors for Cessna trainer planes and I also worked on building B-29 Bombers. Cessna agreed to pay the tuition for anyone wanting to attend college so I took advantage of this free opportunity for a higher education and worked second shift, going to college in the morning.

After returning to Birmingham, I continued to attend college, attending Massey Business College. I then went to work for Bechtel McCombs Parsons Aircraft Company doing modifications on planes. I stayed with this job until the end of WW II. After the war, I went to work for Employers Insurance Company.

In December of 1946, I married James Hasty. We lived in Birmingham for seven months until moving to Albertville, Alabama in 1947. We opened The Jewel Box, a jewelry store, in 1948. In 1955, our son, James, was born and in 1960 our daughter, Janet, was born. My son James and I operated the business until 1990 when I retired. James now owns and operates the business. Janet is the Director of Sales with the Carraway Davie House and Conference Center. She and her husband, Jeremy, live with their daughter, Anna, and son, Ben. Jeremy owns and operates The Model Box, a remote control hobby shop.

Vernelle in 2003

After my retirement, I purchased eight rental houses, which kept me quite busy. I still have two of them and stay as active as I wish, going often to see my grandchildren. I'm also close to my church family at the First Baptist Church of Albertville. I have a Border Collie, Zoe. I am still in good health and drive any place that I wish to go.

WE FOUGHT THE HOME FRONT BATTLE

by Marjorie A. Van Alstine
Coeur d'Alene, Idaho

Marjorie changed her age on her Boeing pass so she could enter the service nightclubs. "But I met no one there like my memory of the handsome 16-year-old Montana cowboy I first met at 10 years old," she says. She later married him!

Yippee! Graduation 1943, and I could leave the valley in Montana where I was raised, and see the world. First stop was Vancouver, Washington, where I worked in a cafeteria, feeding shipyard workers. There I met a girl from Montana who became my friend, roommate, and travel partner.

In the fall of 1943, we left for Seattle, working at Boeing Aircraft, Renton plant as riveters. Two of us replaced rivets that were not acceptable. These were kept on dry ice until warmed by riveting on them. One day I went to the tool room for a fresh supply. My fellow worker reminded me to take the metal container for them. But instead I put them in my shirt pocket. What a mistake! That took much of the cockiness out of 19-year-old me.

After one visit home, we moved on. Next stop was San Francisco and to work at Kaiser Shipyard #4 in Richmond, California. We were apprentice joiners, installing soap and toothbrush holders, shelves, and towel bars in the bathrooms (called heads), and grab bars for hallways, etc. Several in our gang installed locks and keys. Once we locked ourselves in a stateroom for a party. The only thing "edible" was a tobacco plug, so we all took a chew. My, what a sick bunch left that room!

My Montana cowboy friend joined the Marines. One of the ladies in my gang invited me to live with her and her family. (Later I found out that this lady was a kleptomaniac and her husband was a wino.) Their 12-year-old daughter and I celebrated being "teens" together, and it was said that I was like "one of the family."

V-J Day was past and soon the war would be over, so I went to work at Mare Island, a permanent shipyard. Later I returned to Montana, where I married that tall, handsome cowboy.

My war work was challenging, earning sufficient wages for footlong hot dogs in San Francisco. But the greatest part of my life was to come! After my four children were grown and my second husband died, I asked Jesus Christ to be my guide. He gave me four wonderful years as secretary in Hong Kong for Youth for Christ and Training Evangelistic Leadership. I have now seen the world in China, Singapore, Philippines, India, Israel, and Cuba. What a blessed life the God of the universe has given me!

Marjorie more recently

MY ROSIE THE RIVETER EXPERIENCE - WORLD WAR II

by Marion E. Hoines Logan
Eugene, Oregon

Marion Evelyn Hoines Logan in the 1940's

As far back as 1934, my teacher told our class there was a mean man named Hitler, and she wanted all of us to remember this the rest of our lives. I can say I still remember Hitler.

When I was 16, I made a trip to the employment office during my lunch hour. As I entered the employment office, I noticed the employment clerk offering a Civil Service test and physical to become an airplane mechanic. I got the employment form and told the clerk I would be back the next day at noon.

Next day I gave the clerk my filled-out employment form. Several days later I was instructed to be at an appointment to take the Civil Service exam. There were 35 people in the room to take the exam. Two weeks later I was notified to check in at the Stillwater A&M College (now Oklahoma State) and start my mechanic training. We had a half day on-the-job training, and half day in lecture and exam.

After several months I was transferred to Tinker Air Force Base near Oklahoma City, Oklahoma. I was placed in several departments as needed. Some of the duties were using machine tools to grind valves and grind corrosion, sanding valve clamp covers, and storing different engine parts. I lived in downtown Oklahoma City. This required transfers, getting up at 4:30 a.m. and barely getting to base at 7:00 a.m.

Meanwhile, I asked for a transfer to Enid Army Flying School (now called Vance Air Force Base) My parents were divorced and my dad welcomed me. My duties there were in the hangars and doing whatever was needed. We could choose anything on a checklist that someone else hadn't chosen. When we finished, we initialed off and an inspector would check our work. I did a lot of cotter key wiring, tension wiring, replacing cowlings, etc.

I decided I wanted greener pastures and my mom wanted me to come home. I headed for California where the weather was better. I applied and passed the Civil Service exam, and the next day I was assigned to the A & R Building & Hangar (A & R Aerial Repair). I was assigned to the engine o/h school. I also went to aircraft classes once a week for three hours. Some of the duties were to test engine parts by going to the Engine Testing room and testing our engine. If it ran okay, we took it out onto the floor to be later installed on a bomber.

It became almost time for school to start in September. I told my boss I wanted to quit and finish high school. After being out of school for four years, I not only finished high school, but over the years I majored in Business Management and R.E. Management.

MY MOM AS A HOME FRONT ROSIE THE RIVETER
by Marion Evelyn Hoines Logan
Daughter of Pansy Ethelyn Dunkle Hoines

Pansy Dunkle Hoines

My mother, Pansy Ethelyn Dunkle Hoines, was born April 15, 1903 in the Cherokee Nation in Oklahoma before Oklahoma became a state. My ancestors lived in Berlin, when it was Prussia. My great-great-great-grandma was a German Countess and she married a commoner, which made her parents very angry.

Grandma and Grandpa left Prussia via Hamburg, Germany, and eventually arrived at Newton, Iowa, where many of my relatives still live. Many are scattered all over the USA. My great-grandmother married a Hewett and soon my grandmother was born. The government then allowed citizens to acquire 160 acres of land and they moved to the Cherokee Nation area. Soon my mom, the oldest sibling, was born.

My mom graduated Enid High School, and several months later married my dad, Samuel Smith Hoines. Later I was born, their first child, on July 27, 1926. A few years went by, and we heard news about Hitler; it was a very sad time. I was 8 years old when I first understood about him and the mean, bad things he did.

When I was 16, I became a Rosie. Shortly after this, my mom became a Rosie. This makes me an ARRA Rosebud. Mom started working as a riveter at the Bremerton Naval Shipyards at Bremerton, Washington. This was the first time she had worn long pants. She forbade me to wear them, but she wore them for most of the rest of her life.

The war ships came in for repairs. They were docked and all workers were assigned to repair all that needed repairing. There were different damages. The worst was when rooms were blocked off. When opened, it was not a good thing. The smell was terrible and it was very sad.

Mom worked days from January, 1942 until 1945, when the war ended and all the home front workers were laid off. Mom was 4' 11" and being a riveter was a physically demanding job for her, but she enjoyed her role.

Mom passed away in December of 1998, at the age of 97, and is buried at Zillah Cemetery in Zillah, Washington. If she were alive, and knew all the honor of being a Rosie the Riveter, she would be delighted and overjoyed. If there is such a thing as being in Heaven and knowing, I feel she does know.

I WAS WORKING ON THE RAILROAD

by *Marianne T. Mueller Kessler*
Sun City West, Arizona

Marianne Mueller Kessler in 1942

After two years of college, I took a position at a securities and investment firm. In 1943, when I heard that Missouri Pacific Railroad needed office personnel at their headquarters in St. Louis, Missouri to replace men called to military duty, I decided to apply for a job to help the war effort.

I was assigned to the Operations Department, and my job was to obtain sensitive military information, so I was in a classified position. During the day, by telephone from the various station agents, I received the date and time a military or POW (Prisoner Of War) train would arrive on our line, the origin, number of cars, how many men, their destination, and when the train was released to another carrier. Any problems with the equipment, tracks, breakdowns, or delays were also reported to me.

After I had all the needed information, I typed the report in five copies on legal size paper, using a special hard roller on an electric typewriter and special paper and carbon paper. Some days we had 25 or more troop trains moving on our line, and the report took three sheets of paper.

It was mandatory that my report be delivered to the President's office on the 22nd floor by 3:00 p.m. each day. I was not to talk about the troop movements to anyone. Copies of the report were sent only to officers of the railroad. No mimeograph or "ditto" copies were allowed.

I worked there until the men came back from military duty, and was happy to hear from my superiors that they appreciated my reports and loyalty. Also during those years, I joined a group at the DesLoge Hospital, wrapping bandages in the evening for the Red Cross.

I am proud to be a "Rosie," even though I was not a riveter.

Marianne and Milt Kessler in 2003, attending a "prom" after 57 years of marriage!

A SHIPYARD WORKER AND VOLUNTEER NURSE

by
*Velma (Val)
Montgomery Matheny*

Ardmore, Oklahoma

Val Matheny in 1942

I was attending Cameron College in Lawton, Oklahoma when WW II was declared. I married Eden Matheny, a Navy pilot, who had graduated from flight school at Pensacola, Florida. After two weeks of marriage, we went to California, where he left for duty in the Aleutian Islands.

Living in Oakland, California, I was immediately hired to work in the shipyards. I worked the night shift as a timekeeper. Timekeepers spent all the night shift getting the timecards ready for the day shift workers to sign in when they arrived between 7:00 and 8:00 a.m.

Every morning a young boy was selling newspapers to the arriving morning shift. The headline one morning was "Battle Raging in Tunisia." The boy was yelling, "Battle raging in Tennessee!" He was thrilled but oblivious as to the reason he sold all his papers so quickly.

Because of a great need for nurses, I took a hospital

training course for volunteer workers. I volunteered four to six hours on the early morning shift. I was given two meals a day at the hospital.

My job consisted of bathing patients, changing beds, and sitting with seriously ill patients. Having had training to be a teacher, one of my favorite assignments was to sit with young children. One young boy wanted me to come back to his room and play with him, so I often did. After the war, when I was back in Oklahoma, his mother mailed me a cookbook. It is still one of my favorite cookbooks.

Donated blood was in high demand, so if I weighed enough (110 pounds), I would give blood every two months.

The scariest times were nighttime air raid warnings when the shipyard workers were rushed to shelters in the hulks of the ships. One night the rumor was that an enemy submarine had been sighted in the Bay area. Everything had to be quiet and in complete darkness. Not even a cigarette could be lit. Our planes roared into the skies.

The lonely times in California paid off when Eden returned for a few days to the coast after a tour of duty.

Val in 2003

GUN-SMITHING IN WORLD WAR II
by Carolyn E. Fix
Vienna, Virginia

Carolyn E. Fix, Women's Army Corps, 1944

I graduated with a business diploma from New Hartford High School (a suburb of Utica, New York) in June of 1940. But jobs were scarce, so for the next year I took some extra courses at T. R. Proctor High School in Utica. Then in 1942, the National Youth Administration (NYA) offered a four-month (I think) machine shop course to qualify for work in the local war plant. Consequently, I was one of the first four women to work in the Savage Arms Company of Utica, making .30 and .50 caliber Browning machine guns and some parts for the Thompson sub-machine gun.

It was hard operating a hand-mill, spline-mill, and engraver - on my feet for ten hours a day, seven days a week, and then two days off to recuperate. This was called the "swing shift."

Our ride to the plant was in crowded, smoke-filled buses, since no one was allowed to smoke inside the plant. Also, with a thought to my future, I began studying X-ray technology for (I think) two nights a week. I don't recall our wages at the plant, but they were based on piece work and there was no additional overtime pay. The oily wooden floor crunched with bits of metal shavings that worked their way into the soles of our safety shoes. After a year of this work, I became anemic, so I had to quit.

I tried to land a job as an X-ray technician, as I had completed the night course, but everyone required experience. So on November 5, 1943, I joined the Women's Army Corps (WAC) as an X-ray technician and got lots of experience there.

In 1944, Congress gave the troops the GI Bill that would pay for college or other education and guarantee a home mortgage. So when I left the WAC in June, 1948, I went to college and earned BA and MS degrees. In 1960, I bought my first GI Bill home. Thus WW II changed the course of my life and I never went back to X-ray work.

Carolyn in 2001 with her two wire-haired dachshund "granddogs," Winnie the Pooch and Boston Brownie

THE GOLD B-17

by
Phillys Janet Lee Stevenson
Granddaughter of Dora "Bea" Cox Philley

Dora "Bea" Philley at a meeting with fellow workers at McDonnell Douglas, about 1944

Before WW II, on December 22, 1937 to be exact, I was born in Winterhaven, California. My dad was helping build the All-American Canal, which opened southern California to irrigation. Six years later found him finishing woodwork on the Liberty Ships while my grandmother, Dora Cox Philley, was busy building B-17 aircraft. She worked at McDonnell Douglas Corporation, Long Beach, California.

Grandma was a riveter lead man. She faithfully served her country in this capacity for about three years. I can remember going to the plant several times – never in it! It was a fascinating sight! My main question was always, "Why is that big building covered with all that material?" At that time, no matter how the question was answered, I didn't fully understand the meaning of camouflage, nor the importance of Grandma's job.

The sky over Long Beach was filled with small blimps so that enemy planes could not invade our air space. I thought sure that a person could walk across the sky just going from blimp to blimp. Obviously there were not as many blimps in the sky as I remember, but to a young mind it looked like thousands.

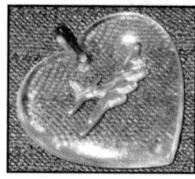

One of my most treasured possessions is a gold, detailed replica of a B-17 encased in a small, clear plastic heart. This was given to Grandma at the completion of one of the planes built under her leadership.

I also have a book that was given to Grandma when she quit working at Douglas. Many people wrote notes to her and autographed it. This book of cartoons is entitled *The Home Front*. It shows that even through this all-too-difficult time, Americans still had a sense of humor. In one cartoon, a character with a patched-up inner tube in his hand is calling his boss from a pay phone by the light of the moon and explaining, "I can't be to work today, cause I ain't got home yesterday YET!"

After one cartoon about standing in line, Edna O'Brien wrote, "Thank goodness the lines are about to end." Some of the signatures are "Tex" R. K. Arnold, Ruth Hansen – R.P.#98, and Brice McCoy. One signature was dated May 29, 1945. It was next to a picture of a worker standing in front of an aircraft looking at his notes and saying, "According to this report, we have an airplane somewhere with three wings and no gas tanks!"

I know that every day must have been a tremendous challenge to every Rosie the Riveter. I do, now, fully understand the meaning of camouflage and the importance of

I LOVED THOSE PLANES
by Mary Hairston Smith Hoaglund
Phoenix, Arizona

Mary Hoaglund in 1943 as she appeared in her Civil Air Patrol ID picture

In 1943, I heard that they were hiring at the airplane modification plant in my hometown of Birmingham, Alabama. At the time I had a six-month-old daughter and I needed a job. As I had always loved airplanes and flying, I went down to apply.

The man that was hiring for the government asked me why I thought I could be an inspector and I told him that I had built model airplanes and could read a blueprint. He said I was hired. That started the job I loved the most in my lifetime. Although the war was awful, I sure loved working on those airplanes.

I actually started before the plant was opened. There was just a shed, and the first three or four planes were under that shed. We worked on them there until the plant was finished. In the beginning, we inspected B-24's, then after about a year I inspected B-24's, "The Liberator," B-29's, "The Super Fortress," and P-38's, "Lightening." I loved being around those planes. Whenever I got an extra $10, I went and took flying lessons on a Piper Cub J3.

My older brother, Robert, also worked at the plant. He was an Armament Leadman and sometimes I got to inspect his work. We both took great pride in our jobs.

I always took something home for my young daughter in my lunch box, sometimes a candy bar or part of my lunch. I never missed a day of work, but once I was five minutes late. I had been up flying and there was a storm in Florida. They were bringing planes in from other airports so I could not land. That was the only time I was late.

In 2001, I had one of my dreams come true. I got to go up for a flight on the B-24 owned by the Collins Foundation. Its name was the "Dragon and Its Tail." Also, I became a member of the American Rosie the Riveter Association in the Sun City, Arizona chapter, which is the largest in the nation. What a great group of gals.

During those years I also got letters from some of the squadrons that had received the planes that I had worked on. I sent cookies and candies to them. They were in Italy and they told me that they named one of their planes after me. After the war, I never heard from any of them again.

I worked there from January, 1943 until October, 1945. I was among the first to be hired and one of the last to leave. I have never forgotten it!

Mary at age 80 with one of her model airplanes, as she appeared in an article about Rosies in The Arizona Republic *in 2004*

AUNTIE EL,
A ROSIE THE RIVETER

by Ella M. Tauzin Fortner of Biloxi, Mississippi
As told to her niece, Lanelle Hanke

Ella Marie and Henry Charles Fortner about 1940 (left) and in 1996, the year of their 60th wedding anniversary

During WW II, Mae and I went to get jobs as riveters. Mae would do the riveting and I would do the bucking. We worked at Consolidated Aircraft Builders in New Orleans, Louisiana after six weeks of training.

After training, we went to the plant and we got in the plane. They were tight quarters. Mae couldn't get in those little places. Sometimes I would be lying on my stomach in the bottom of the plane. Sometimes the place would be so small, all you could get in there would be your head and arms, with your legs way up like a V. With all that noise, I was nervous, you know! My doctor said that I would have to do something else. So I went over in the Parts Department where I would burr little pieces of metal. We would get the burrs off with a file. Then we would drill holes in some of the pieces on different little parts of the plane.

We worked on the 4:00 p.m. to 12:00 shift at night. When we got off, we rode a bus home and it would really be late. One night a man was going to get off the bus and Mae saw him take out a knife, so she went up and sat behind the driver.

She said, "Bud," (Mae called all men Bud if she didn't know their name), "Bud, this man's coming to get off and he's got a knife in his hand." So the driver was ready. The man had tried to rob the driver two times before and someone saw him both times. From then on, we had a security guard ride with us.

Let me tell you about the planes. PBY's had two bubbles. They were the only seaplanes that had the bubbles on them. The bubbles were up there for the gunners. Sometimes they were used to rescue people.

Right across the street from where we worked was a prisoner of war camp. The prisoners would be out in the back yard. There was a big fence, but we'd see them all the time. I don't know where they were from. We were about a block from Ponchartrain.

I didn't work too long, about eight or nine months. Then Henry came home and I went with him. He went to a lifeboat station down in Galveston, Texas. I went there with him and I loved it. I could have stayed there forever. But I also missed home. Henry asked if I wanted to follow the job to Mexico and I said, "No, I want to go home." So we came home.

Note from El's niece: Aunt El Marie Tauzin Fortner passed away on July 4, 3½ months after giving me her story. She had received her American Rosie the River Association membership certificate and was so proud of it. I will always be grateful that you started this organization and that I heard about it in time for my aunt to be a part of it.

THE WOODEN LEG

by
Jean Rubin
Meyers Levitas

Baltimore, Maryland

Jean Levitas at age 18 in 1943 in Baltimore

It's 1943, and we are at war. I'm 18 years old and graduating from high school, trained in the commercial course to work in an office, typing and taking shorthand. I turn on the radio in the morning and the news is full of our losses and the many planes being shot down. It is urgent that our armed forces get airplane replacements as soon as they can.

I decided it was patriotic to go to work in a defense plant, rather than an office. I lived in a suburban area and it took me one and three-quarters of an hour and three transfers on the streetcar to get to Eastern Aircraft, General Motors plant on Broening Highway in Baltimore to apply for a job. There were no buses then and 18-year-olds did not own cars, plus with gas being rationed, you couldn't afford it.

I was hired and went to a training class for six weeks to

learn how to rivet. I learned how to handle a drill, learned all about different drill bits, learned what a clecoe was and clecoe pliers, and how to handle a bucking bar against the rivets.

I passed the test and went on the conveyor production line. Eastern Aircraft was building the rear fuselage of the fighter plane. Production in June of 1943 was 170 planes a month. By 1945, towards the end of the war, production had increased to 300 planes a month.

We had to follow safety rules. There were no windows in the rear fuselage of the plane, so when an employee was working up on the ladder on the outside of the plane, it was his or her responsibility to alert the employees working on the inside that he or she was there.

Sure enough, a young man who was 4F was up on the ladder checking rivets and did not look inside to see if there was a driller working. I was inside drilling and assembling the brackets to be riveted, when my drill went through the metal and got stuck. I kept on pulling and pulling on the drill to come out, but it didn't budge. Suddenly from overhead a voice says, "Hey Jean, I'm damn lucky you just drilled into my wooden left leg and not my good right leg."

Well, he was lucky, but he was also at fault because he neglected to check for workers inside the rear fuselage. The drill had gotten caught onto his pant leg and went all the way through to his wooden leg. We all had a good laugh, and thank goodness he wasn't hurt.

Jean, age 78, at the national ARRA convention in Baltimore in 2004

WORLD WAR II MEMORIES
by Velora L. S. S. Anderson
Bessemer, Alabama

Velora Anderson (left) and a fellow worker, on their way to work in 1942, wearing safety shoes, tan coveralls, and hats

In 1940, I left our family's Illinois farm to work in St. Louis, Missouri. At that time, single women were chaperoned, so a cousin found me a boarding room in a beautiful old mansion whose housemother provided meals and loving care. Residents had various occupations, some hoping for better-paying or more interesting work.

In December 1940, the U. S. government contracted with the United States Cartridge Company to build and operate the St. Louis Ordnance Plant, called "the Greatest Small Arms Plant in the Military History of the Nation." Ironically, the first ammunition came off line December 8, 1941, the day after the Japanese attacked Pearl Harbor.

Our housemother arranged for us to volunteer at a nearby USO. We helped servicemen telephone or write letters home, listened to their fun and homesick stories, served food, and danced with them when name bands of that era came to the USO. Dating was not permitted.

Several of us applied at the St. Louis Ordnance Plant. Telegrams assigned dates to appear for health, skill, and strength tests. Subsequent telegrams gave dates to report to work. Mine arrived in early 1942, to start work as a machinist operator of a pocketing machine, which stamped the powder packet into brass casings for tracer bullets. The huge, tall, oblong machines were electrically powered but manually controlled, with a large, heavy foot brake that required hard, quick jumps to stop it. This was difficult for women, but we did it, wearing safety shoes and glasses, tan coveralls and caps. My first weekly paycheck was $22.04.

One day my machine stopped The millwright arrived, carefully turned the power off, and climbed down into the area where the huge punch rod glided through a track toward the brass casing. As he worked, I saw the rod slowly begin to shift and start moving toward him. I jumped down hard on the brake; the rod slowed, but didn't stop. He lost three fingers on his right hand, but at least he didn't lose his arm or his life. I wondered if a man could have controlled the machine better.

It was a special time, everyone working together to help free the world, and it opened the work world to women. My fiancé, a member of the First Armored School, Fort Knox, Kentucky, was happy and proud that I was helping produce ammunition to defeat our enemies.

We married in August, 1942. I joined him at Ft. Knox in 1943 and then followed him during his more than 20-year Army career, across the USA and to Japan with our daughter .

America is so blessed. Our flag waving in the air makes me so very proud to be an American and a Rosie!

MY WORK FOR THE WAR EFFORT
by Anna L. Johnson
Wichita, Kansas

Anna Johnson, age 63, at a party given in her honor at the time of her retirement in 1986

When the war started, Boeing had training school for sheet metal workers, so I signed up for it. They paid 50 cents an hour to get a month's training. Then you went to the big plant.

I got a chance to go to work for Aero Parts. That's where I met my friend, Cathy Terrell, with whom I still keep in touch. We worked there for three years until they closed. My home was at Harper, Kansas, where we lived on a farm. Beech Aircraft had a small plant in Harper, so I worked there for eight months.

Then I went to Denver, Colorado to work at Gates Rubber Plant, but I didn't stay very long. I went back home and worked at Boeing for a while. In the meantime, Cessna bought the old Areo Parts building, and I was hired there. It was closer for me to drive and stay at home. I had a load of riders for ten years, for the 100 miles round trip to work.

My father passed away in 1962, so my mother and I moved to Wichita, Kansas, closer to my job. I worked on B-29 wings and B-52 stabilizers for several years. It was hard work but paid well, so I stayed. I was never laid off, and I worked on any planes that Cessna built.

I always worked in production. My last job, when I retired, was on their Citation 650 Business Jet that they were building at that time. I retired in 1986 with 36½ years, so all together, I have close to 40 years in aircraft work. I guess that makes me a "Rosie the Riveter," for I sure did drive a lot of rivets.

My youngest sister was a Rosie, too. She worked for Boeing until she married an Air Force man and then moved a lot.

You should see the Cessna buildings now, out by the airport. They are big, white buildings on each side of the highway and have pretty landscapes. They still have the Cessna name and make the same beautiful jets. I was able to go up in one before I retired.

Being a Rosie was hard work, but I would do it all over again. I am past 80 now, and I am proud of my work for the war effort.

PERHAPS THE YOUNGEST B-29 RIVETER
by Jean L. Kowalski Lund
Sun City Grand, Arizona

Jean Kowalski Lund in 1945 in Seattle, Washington

I became a riveter on B-29 bombers because of the extreme poverty for many of us during the Great Depression of the 1930's. From the age of eight, working in the fields, I knew I wanted a chance for a better life. WW II gave me that opportunity.

I turned 16 in April, 1944. I got a job in a creamery, cracking eggs for powdered eggs for the Army. I saved enough money to buy a train ticket to Seattle, Washington, with $38 left over! Fearing for my safety, my parents would not give their permission for me to go. So the day before I was planning to leave, I packed my few items of clothing in a cardboard box and took it to my girlfriend's apartment. I then bought my ticket to Seattle. I asked my mother if I could stay overnight with my friend. At 3:00 a.m., I boarded the Great Northern train from Moorhead, Minnesota. The train was filled with young sevicemen on their way overseas. I became so lonely and homesick that I spent most of the trip on the platform between rail cars, crying, or in the restroom with stomach cramps.

Arriving in Seattle after 36 hours on the train, I was devastated to find Boeing had an 18-year-old minimum. Since I was just 16, someone told me about Puget Sound Sheet Metal works, a company that manufactured wing and tail sections for Boeing B-29's. I was fortunate to be hired.

We were allowed two 15-minute rest breaks and a 30-minute lunch break. As soon as the whistle blew, some of us would lie down on the wooden pallets and immediately fall asleep. Beginning wages were 82½ cents an hour as bucker. After three months, 92½ cents as a B riveter, and 110½ cents as a grade A riveter Those were big, big wages back then.

I had found a sleeping room with a hot plate in a nice lady's home for $5.00 a week. Several months later, my mother decided to come to Seattle to work at Boeing. She brought my younger sister, and I found us an apartment in a new housing project.

One of my jobs as a riveter left long spirals of metal about three inches long. One time I made a spider's body with some pie dough, using raisins for eyes and the metal spirals for legs. When my mother opened what she thought was a jewelry gift and saw the spider, she screamed and almost fainted. Then she saw the humor in it and named it Adam. Many years later, we kids found it in a closet. When my mother opened the case, she screamed again. We all laughed, and it brought back many memories.

I never regretted my decision to leave home and work in a war plant. After the war ended, I completed high school and went on to college. The war was hell but it made men and women of the "Greatest Generation."

MY "ROSIE" STORY
by Maxine Rose Rice Zimmerman
Piqua, Ohio

Maxine Zimmerman in the 1940's

As high school seniors in 1941, we were very aware of the threats of war that surrounded us daily. But on December 7, 1941, those threats became a stunning reality. Friends and I were leaving a movie in Tippecanoe, Ohio and saw a boy waving newspapers shouting, "Extra – Pearl Harbor has been bombed – we are at war."

I had never seen an Extra before, and had no idea where Pearl Harbor was, but I knew that our world had just fallen apart.

I started working at Lears Aviation in Piqua, Ohio right after graduation, inspecting the winding of armatures and stators. Later that year I started working at Aeroproducts

Aviation in Vandalia, Ohio. There I was trained to operate a huge 15-foot milling machine. I milled gears for aircraft propellers.

In January, 1942, I got married and continued to work at Aeroproducts until our son was born in October, 1942. My husband was drafted in December, 1942, and after Basic Training, was sent to Fort Bliss at El Paso, Texas. My friend's husband was also stationed at Fort Bliss, so we packed our two baby boys and followed. Since her baby wasn't well, we agreed that I would work and pay expenses while she cared for our little boys. I got two jobs. One was at a USO canteen, and the second was at the popular downtown Chinese Café. Both were very hard work, long hours, but fun. The Café paid $1.00 per day plus tips and the Canteen, I think 50 cents. The service men loved both places and they were always packed. Texas rangers and movie stars also gathered at the Café. That's where I met John Wayne while he was making a movie near El Paso.

When my husband was shipped overseas for D-Day, I went back to work on aircraft propellers in Aeroproducts Aviation in Vandalia, Ohio, assembling propeller hubs. I jet-washed the hubs in a spraying booth, moved the hubs to the line (they weighed 90 pounds), then assembled the gears and other parts into the hubs. As I remember, the tolerance for the gear clearance was $1/10,000^{th}$ of an inch. Aeroproducts propellers are now displayed at Wright-Patterson Air Force Museum at Dayton, Ohio.

Thanks to President Franklin Roosevelt and the GI Bill, my husband came home in 1945 to learn a good trade and on Christmas Day, 1948, we were blessed with a baby daughter.

I am thankful to have been a part of the 6 million women replacing men on the home front so more soldiers could fight Germany and Japan as they aspired to destroy America.

A WORLD WAR II ROMANCE

by Ora Caroline Leonard Sellers
Lexington, North Carolina

Jim and Caroline Sellers in 1945

In 1939, I left my hometown of Lexington, North Carolina and spent nearly a year nearby in Ellerbe, North Carolina at the National Youth Association. The first lady, Eleanor Roosevelt, arrived there one day to inspect the work we were doing. I cherish the snapshot I took of her at the workshop where we made gloves, bedding, etc.

In 1942, I began work as a riveter at the Glenn L. Martin plant in Middle River, Maryland. I worked on the outboard section of the B-26 Marauder under my boss, "Red" Hughes. We worked in pairs; while I riveted, my partner would hold the steel bar against the sheet metal that we were joining. If the rivet was not flat and even, I had to drill it out. We wore coveralls and covered our hair with scarves or bandanas to keep from having our hair yanked out in the motors. We proudly earned several "E" awards and pins for our excellent work.

One thing that stands out among my memories at Martin plant was seeing the monstrous seaplane, the Spruce Goose. It belonged to Howard Hughes, the movie director.

On my first night there, one of the guys on the crew walked up to me with a little whistle. I turned away and started working. I thought it best to avoid wolfish men on the job. Little did I dream I would become married to this guy!

When I jammed a broken drill bit into my hand, Jim was waiting outside the infirmary where I had treatment. We eventually dated, but not steadily at first.

Jim's family relocated from Hollidaysburg, Pennsylvania to Dundalk, Maryland. His mother had two sons and one daughter already in service when Jim was drafted in 1945. The day Jim gave me my engagement ring, we learned of the death of President Roosevelt. Jim never knew that I went to Fort Bragg to turn down an offer of marriage from another serviceman that had been made while I was home on leave from Martin.

We were married by Chaplain Brooks on June 23, 1945, in a little chapel at Camp Wheeler in Macon, Georgia. Thus began 55 years of marriage blessed by three children — Jimmy, Michael, and Georgeanna. At this writing, Jim and Michael are deceased.

WANT TO DO MORE
by Theresa Dypsky Posko
Pasadena, Maryland

Theresa Dypsky Posko (left) and her partner at work at Glenn L. Martin in the 1940's

We were a family of 15, and I was the only girl with 11 brothers. I saw three of my brothers go off to the war, one in the Army and two in the Merchant Marines. I thought, "I want to do more!"

I was 17 years old and not yet old enough to work, so I did what any determined young girl would do – I changed my birth certificate! I was then able to be hired at Glenn L. Martin, Middle River Plant. I started working as a riveter in 1944 for Glenn L. Martin at Plant 2 on the B-26 aircraft.

I was assigned to work on the wing and fuselage of the plane. The women were paired in two's, and while another girl would back the rivet with a heavy bar, I would use a special gun to seal it. I felt that I, and all the girls, were making a difference and helping America at this time of need.

During this experience, I made some distinct memories. One memory is of many celebrities and movie stars rallying at Glenn L. Martin to sell Liberty Bonds. Another memory I'll never forget was a crew returning from combat on a B-26 airplane. I felt proud!

After about 14 months at Glenn L. Martin, I decided to leave and work for Eastern Aircraft on the swing shift. The off shift really appealed to me at that time. Little did I know (sometimes things are just meant to be) it would be then that I met my future husband, Henry Posko, Sr. He worked at Maryland Drydock on ships. We both worked the night shift and met on a blind date after one of our shifts. We were married in 1948, and have been happily married for 56 years. We share 5 children and 17 grandchildren.

Yes, I wanted to do more and I am proud to be a part of American history, but I believe I gained as much as I gave!

Theresa with her husband, Henry, and their five children

MY YEARS AS A ROSIE

by
Gladys Owenby Donohue

Garden Grove, California

Gladys Owenby Donohue in Oak Ridge, Tennessee in the 1940's

When WW II began and the young men were called into the military, many jobs were left unfilled. That is when the women stepped in. My first job was at Van Ralte Hosiery Mill in Blue Ridge, Georgia, as a machinist's helper. Each machine had a male machinist with a female helper at each end. We made silk hosiery and the mill ran 24/7.

After leaving Van Ralte, I worked in Atlanta, Georgia, for a short time in a banking clearing house and in the Learner's warehouse. My brother, Cecil, was stationed in Aberdeen, Maryland, and he invited me to come live with him and his wife, Carol. I had no problem getting a job at the Aberdeen Proving Grounds in the mail department.

From Maryland we moved to Texas, where I worked in the PX on base. From Texas, we transferred back to Maryland and I worked in the airplane factory, testing parts. For security reasons, I was required to work in a wire cage in the middle of the factory.

Soon my brother was shipped overseas. His wife went home to California and I went home to Georgia. Once there, I heard they were hiring in Oak Ridge, Tennessee, and I was on the go again! My sister, Hazel Owenby Harper, and I traveled to Tennessee. Oak Ridge, "The City Behind the Fence," wasn't much different from what I was accustomed to – security, badges, gates, etc. I had no problem getting clearance. I was simply transferred from Maryland, and was assigned to an office as Clerk I in the Y12 Plant, working with ten other women.

All our work was done in a large vault. We did filing, keypunch, and numbering requisitions. Every piece of paper was in code, including the keypunch material – nothing made sense. In August, 1945, when the A-Bomb was dropped on Japan, we learned, along with the world, why we were in Oak Ridge and what we did there.

After the war ended, they began scaling down operations. I stayed until I was terminated in February, 1947. Looking back now, I can acknowledge and appreciate the contributions we "Rosies" made to the war effort.

Gladys Donohue in 2004

ROSIE THE RIVETER
by Darlene P. DeMars Smith
Lacey, Washington

Darlene DeMars Smith in 1943

I lived in Minnesota, was out of high school, and had no money for college. My name at that time was Darlene P. DeMars. I heard that the Boeing Aircraft Company factory in Wichita, Kansas was hiring ladies to work in their production lines. I borrowed $25 from my sister and bought a bus ticket to Kansas.

I arrived there late at night in a howling snowstorm. The next day, I applied at the factory. I was hired, took a physical examination, and began work the next morning at 6:00 a.m The date was January 1, 1943. For one week, I attended blueprint school and riveting training before going to the factory as "Rosie the Riveter." I was assigned as a sheet metal worker to prepare and rivet aluminum pieces to each other and to the structure of the airplanes. I was dressed in coveralls and wore a bandana on my head. The rule was that all hair was to be covered.

WW II was in progress and women were needed to work to replace the men that were off to war protecting our country. The men were very heroic and so were we women on the home front! Our country pulled together like it had never done before.

In the twentieth century, women won the right to pursue paid work outside of the home. To do so, they broke down the barriers and shattered assumptions.

I was one of the women who worked very hard assembling the great B-29 bomber, the *Enola Gay*. It had a wing span of 104 feet.

I was there when the first B-29 was rolled out of the factory and down the runway to go to war. What a day that was for a , 19-year-old, 98-pound, 5' 1" girl!

I was strong and was a hard worker. We worked 10-hour days, 7 days a week for many long periods. I was used for many of the jobs inside the wings because I was very strong and small. What a great memory it seems now, 59 years later.

Darlene at a DAR meeting in Washington state in 2002

HAPPY TIMES AT BOEING
by Charlotte L. Bumgardner
Sun City, Arizona

Charlotte and Henry Bumgardner in 1943

My husband Henry and I were newlyweds in 1941. We had only been married seven months when he enlisted. Henry was working at Boeing Aircraft in Wichita, Kansas at the time. He was working in the Allocation Department. That is the area where the books are kept. His job was to keep track of things in the stock room and be responsible for bookkeeping and accounting.

Henry enlisted into the Air Force as a Private in April of 1942. When he came home from the war in 1946, he was a First Lieutenant.

When Henry went into the service, I began working in the same department where he had been. My job was working as a secretary for Mr. Wiley Chastain. The job consisted of writing letters to various companies, bookkeeping ,and doing inventory.

Boeing was a company that worked 24 hours a day. My shift was at night and I rode a bus to and from work. The bus was usually full of women.

I remember that at the end of our shift on the way home, many of us would sing the popular songs of that era. We all enjoyed the singing and it gave us an extra feeling of camaraderie. I often led the singing. We sang all the old favorites like "Shine On, Shine On Harvest Moon," "I've Been Working on the Railroad," and "Billy Boy, Billy Boy."

At that time, Boeing was one of the largest companies making airplanes. It was responsible for producing the B-17 and B-29 bombers. Women came out in full force producing these aircrafts because we were desperately needed. We were all very proud of our husbands and family members overseas. We all wanted to do whatever we could to do our part toward freedom and the war effort.

One of the things I would joke with my husband Henry about later was the fact that he only made 90 cents an hour compared to my pay, which was 95 cents an hour.

Many years have passed since then. We raised four children, and will celebrate 63 good years of marriage this October. Truly God has blessed us with many fond memories of a life lived with love, honest work, and laughter.

SHIPYARD WELDER
by Florence E. Wilkinson Lane
Portland, Oregon

Florence Wilkinson Lane (front row, third from left) with other members of her three-plate welding crew

December, 1941 found our family living in the woods north of Grants Pass, Oregon, in a building that was originally the cookhouse of an old mining operation. Even though we had no electricity or running water, my mother cooked for a 10-man testing crew throughout the summer, and she baked bread every day. My father did construction work at Camp White near Medford, and came home weekends. My sister Mary was married, and my brother Chuck was away from home with the Oregon National Guard.

Dad was home one weekend when our neighbor drove up and shouted, "Turn on your radio. The Japanese just bombed Pearl Harbor." I will never forget that day and the changes it brought to our lives.

Chuck's company was called into active duty and would be shipped to the south Pacific. Dad, Mom, and I moved into an apartment in Medford, and I enrolled in welding school. I was the only girl in the class. My instructor was proud of my progress and showed off some of my plates saying, "My girl did this."

Shortly before Christmas, we moved to an apartment in Portland, Oregon. Dad and I applied for work at the Swan Island shipyard, where tankers were being built. Dad was hired immediately as a steamfitter on the outfitting dock. Because I was still a teenager, I needed a permission slip. I took the test and was hired as a three-plate welder.

Our move to Portland proved to be quite expensive, with special clothing, union dues, etc. We did not get paid until after Christmas, so our Christmas dinner consisted of red beans. After we were paid, Mom stocked the cupboard, packed lunches, figured out ration books, saved grease, and stood in lines for scarce items.

I had to cover all my hair with a bandana under my padded welder's cap, and wear heavy leather clothes and steel-toed boots when working. Later I was moved to the "afterpeak" assembly jig. The job was exciting, even though it was noisy and dirty. I still remember the thrill of watching the first tanker launching. It was hard for me to believe that I had a small part in building that huge ship.

Florence more recently

Years later, when going through the Panama Canal on a cruise, I saw four tankers waiting to go through. I thought, "Could one of those be one we built?" I heard they had sold

THE GOOD OLD DAYS
by Loraine Sublett Hamilton
Durham, California

Loraine Hamilton at age 18 in the 1940's (left) and at age 78 in 2004

Some may consider the "good old days" as nothing more than a short memory or a vivid imagination. But I look back to when times were hard, money was scarce, and a war was going on to be some of the happiest of my life.

In 1943, my parents were suffering from very hard times. We were living in Arkansas where work was scarce. There had been a terrible Depression and a World War had started. My parents had decided to move to Los Angeles, California to look for work in the shipyards.

They rented a place on the Imperial Highway. I was 17 years old at that time and made a serious, but unwise, decision to quit school and go to work. I say unwise, as I never returned to get a better education. I felt I had an obligation to go to work. I had to attend school on Saturdays due to my age, but I was able to obtain employment in what I believe to be El Segundo. The plant I worked in was called Marmon Products. It made small parts for aircrafts. This was mainly handwork, with lots of burring on the sharp edges and many other things. I also learned to spot weld and run other small machines, and I did some riveting. I had to leave home early and walk a distance to the streetcar, which I would ride for the several miles to the plant.

My father was a very strict and deeply religious man. He advised me that I could not wear slacks to work. He felt this was sinful, so I was told to wear a dress until I got to work and then change into slacks. When I finished working, I was to change back into a dress before returning home. He was very strict about this.

After living in the Los Angeles area for a year or so, my parents decided to return to their farm in Arkansas. Although I was 18 at this time, I decided to go with them.

Finding no work in the area of northern Arkansas, I soon left for Wichita, Kansas to live with some cousins and their grandmother. Soon after, I was hired at Beech Aircraft. There I was taught to make the tip of the wing for the aircraft. We fit sheet metal over what was called a jib.

I loved my work and I stayed with Beech Aircraft until the war was over. After the war, my high school sweetheart returned from the south Pacific where he had been serving in the Navy. We married, and now have four wonderful children.

I am proud of the work I did to help out in the war. I feel it was a very small part of what I could do for the boys overseas. I would do it again if called on to do so. In those "good old days" we all did what we could to insure what we now enjoy, and sometimes take for granted, in this wonderful country known as these United States of America. Our boys fought and died for our freedom. We should cherish it.

OLE ROSIE OF WORLD WAR II
by Dr. Frances Tunnell Carter
Birmingham, Alabama

Frances Tunnell Carter in the 1940's (left), and walking with her husband, John, in a 5K run on the day of their 50th wedding anniversary in 1996

Yes, even if I am an Ole Rosie now, I can remember WW II and becoming a real Rosie rookie. I was 20-year-old Frances Tunnell, and had no husband, no children, and not too many responsibilities. I had been helping Daddy on our farm near Pontotoc, Mississippi, had finished two years of college and taught school for one year (52 children – kindergarten through second grade – all in one room!).

Then in April, 1943, I decided I wanted to get more involved in the war effort. I realized that if I had been a boy I'd already be in the military, and what I really wanted to do was enlist in the WAVES or WACS. But my mom said "no" to that, so I opted for a defense job. I left rural

Pontotoc County and came to Birmingham Alabama, to take a job in the sheet metal department of Bechtel McCombs Parsons Airplane Modification Center.

I was assigned work as a riveter, and sometimes a bucker, on B-29 fuselages. In my wildest dreams I had never imagined this. In fact, I had never heard of buckers and riveters before. But I was thrilled to be working at something to help win the war and bring the boys back.

Our plant had worked on B-24's earlier, but by the time I arrived they were all B-29's – ten big bays of them! They had been built elsewhere but flown to Birmingham for finishing. We Rosies (and a few good men who had special skills or were over-aged or physically unable to serve in the military) would complete the hydraulic and electrical systems, as well as the interiors and some parts of the fuselages. When the planes left us, they were ready for combat. I have been told that 1/6 of all B-29's that were produced during WW II were finished in our plant.

Safety rules were strictly enforced, including dress codes: coveralls or slacks, rubber-soled shoes, hairnets or head coverings, and goggles when drilling or riveting. I tried to comply rigidly, but somehow one day I got a load of aluminum dust in my eye. They whisked me off to the doctor, but it wasn't any big deal. They flushed my eye with water and sent me back to work. But to me it was quite an event – my first visit to a doctor in my whole life! Daddy had some medical training, and he had delivered me and taken care of my needs until then.

As the war wound down, I returned to finish college at the University of Southern Mississippi near Camp Shelby. I worked as a volunteer, entertaining soldiers at the USO. Many of them were returning from overseas to be mustered out. Among them was my special paratrooper, who arrived there from Europe in December, 1945, in time for us to be married in March of 1946 and to live happily together ever after – so far!

TWO YEARS I'LL NEVER FORGET
by Joan Sargent Clayberger
Woodburn, Oregon

Joan S. Clayberger (on right) "on the job in 1943"

In June of 1943, I had just finished my junior year at Woodburn High School. I needed a summer job, so a friend and I got on the bus and went to Portland to the shipyard there (Oregon Shipbuilding Corporation). We were hired as shipwrights' helpers, a nice name for the clean-up crew.

We rode about 50 miles each way on a bus with other shipyard workers, mostly older men.

We worked on the ships from start to launching. During my senior year, I worked weekends and any days we had off from school. After graduation, I trained to be a burner and I did that until the war was over.

I still have my hard hat, my picture badge, and an uncashed check for $.33 (all that was left of my pay after a war bond drive). I have a corsage of saving stamps, given to me when I was asked to present the flowers for a ship launching. I also have pictures of the launching.

It was all an experience that I will never forget.

Joan with one of her great-grandsons, "still on the job in 2004"

THE STORY OF A ROSIE
by *Hazel Mae Hatchett Belcher*
Oklahoma City, Oklahoma
As told to her daughter, Donna Belcher Young

Hazel Mae Belcher's grave marker celebrates her service to the US as a Rosie the Riveter.

I met my husband of 61 years, Morris Franklin Belcher, during my senior year of high school. We were married on November 26, 1941, in Oklahoma City, Oklahoma, just 11 days before the attack on Pearl Harbor. Morris was drafted in 1942 and worked as a glider mechanic.

When Morris was assigned to bases for training, I followed him as permitted, and cherished my time with him. Our last night together before he left was spent on the grass with a fence between us, holding hands when the guards weren't looking, talking about our dreams and future.

During the war, I lived with my good friend, Rosalee Brooks, who was also a newlywed with a husband in the service. We shared a small apartment and were both hired at Tinker Air Force Base in Oklahoma City.

Rosalee and I became very close and helped each other through the tough times. The shortages and rationing of food, gasoline, and other goods were a minor inconvenience to us. We had grown up during the Depression, so we knew how to get by. We knew our troops needed everything we could send them. We recycled anything that was needed.

When word went out that Tinker Air Force Base and Douglas Aircraft were hiring women, Rosalee and I applied. I became a spot welder. The pay was good, which meant we could save more of our husbands' checks and our own, so when the war was over we could get our lives off to a better start. I got the "We Can Do It!" attitude.

Once I was asked by a General if I would like a tour of a finished B-29. This was unusual. I took the tour, feeling something of a big shot and not realizing what this particular bomber was destined to do. Some time later I was told in great secrecy that the plane was the *Enola Gay*, the plane that dropped the Hiroshima bomb.

By the time the war was over, I was more than ready for it to end, as we all were. Getting my husband back home, safe and sound, was one of the best times of my life. After the war, I went to work for a bank and an oil company. We saved our money and bought a new home in 1948. Our first child, Donna Sue, was born in March, 1950, followed by our son, William Roy, in September, 1953.

During the war, I learned a great deal about myself and others. The most valuable thing I learned and would like to pass on is that no matter how bad things get, if we stick together, treat each other with dignity and respect, and learn to love one another, we can get through anything. Love and faith will always sustain us.

Note from Hazel Mae's daughter: These stories were told to me by my precious mother, Hazel Mae Belcher. We lost her on April 27, 2003. These are wonderful memories that my mom passed on to me and I will pass on to my parents' grandchildren and great-grandchildren.

A REAL PISTOL PACKIN' MAMMA
by Florence V. Russell Field
Camarillo, California

Left: Inspectors Gladys Bresslin and Florence Russell (on right) in 1943. Right: Florence and Corporal James Ray Russell in 1944, while he was home from the Aleutians and before he left for Italy.

It was 1942, and there was a war going on. I was 27, and still single, teaching in a small town down by the Mexican border. There were numerous training camps for the military nearby. One night I found Mr. Right, and after 3½ months, we got married.

When he was sent overseas a month later, I decided to return to Los Angeles, where I had grown up, and do something on the home front. In the town of Burbank was the Lockheed Aircraft Company, which was turning out the P-38 fighter planes. Since Burbank was just over the hill from my home, it was a convenient place to get to. Luckily, there was an opening in an office in a huge hangar, where the P-38's were put through the final inspection before being released to go "into service."

What I didn't know was that there were no women working in that huge hangar – yet. I was still relatively young, and still had a fairly decent figure, so the first day I showed up on the job there were "wolf whistles" coming from all over that cavernous plant. Finally, I found my office and met my new boss, who happened to be Polish. He was so much fun, it made it a pleasure to go to work. But we did work seriously. Little by little, as I typed up the "squawk sheets" the Inspectors brought me, I began to learn the semantics of those planes, which, years later, I learned the Germans called the "fork-tail devils."

One day a lovely young lady came to work in our department, but instead of putting her at a typewriter, the boss put her "out on the line." She was to be an Inspector! But when we learned she had a pilot's license, we knew she had to be qualified. Gladys and I became good friends, and one day she said to me, "Flo, why don't you come out on the line and be an Inspector with me?" But the only parts of the planes with which I was familiar were the names I had typed from the Inspector's squawk sheets. She assured me that our job would be to see that all the loose equipment was there and properly stowed. Our final stamp went on the plane's documents so it could be released into service in the various war zones. Working there by the runway where the planes took off to be tested or flown away, or where they were coming in from all over the world to be repaired or modified, was exciting. We got to know the test pilots, so working there was a privilege.

One of the most important items in the loose equipment was a Verry Pistol, which shot a strong beam of light high into the air in case the pilot was shot down and needed to be rescued. So that is why I was a "Pistol Packin' Mamma" (a song popular in those days) instead of a Rosie the Riveter.

ROSIE THE RIVETER
by Gloria Wassung Morrissette
Belchertown, Massachusetts

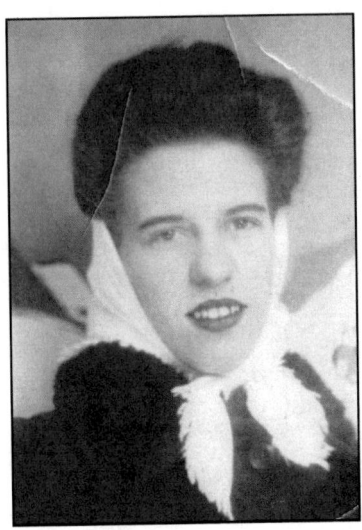 

Gloria Morrissette in the 1940's (left) and in 2004

My maiden name was Gloria Wassung. I was 17 years old on December 6, 1941, one day before the Japanese bombed Pearl Harbor. The following year, I quit school and went to work in Building 104 at the Springfield Armory in Springfield, Massachusetts to help the war effort. I worked from 11:00 p.m. to 7:00 a.m.

I worked on the milling machines on what they called the gas cylinders, the part that goes on top of the gun to hold the bayonet. The name of the gun was the Grand Rifle. I ran a drill press with 16 drills at one time, and I had to keep up with it and couldn't let it stop. Also, I ran the reamers and the profilers.

The machines were going 24 hours a day without stopping. You could burn your hands on the machines because they were red hot. While we were working, they would let us have soda to drink, because our throats would get very dry from the heat of the machines. For our break, we had only 20 minutes to eat. There was no time to waste. We ate outside in the fresh air at 3:00 in the morning.

I lived in North Wilbraham, Massachusetts. When I first got the job, I had to travel 32 miles a day, 16 miles each way. Each night I had to walk the first mile and wait for the bus to take me to work. After working a full shift, I would take the bus for 15 miles and walk the mile to get home. I was very dedicated, and I thought the job was very interesting. At the time, I brought home over $45 a week. That was good money in those days. One time I worked three weeks in a row without a day off. After we moved to Chicopee, Massachusetts, I was lucky enough to have a driver to take me to work.

We had to wear hairnets so that our hair would not get caught in the machines. The girls started to wear long pants then because skirts would get caught in the machines. The few men who worked with us were called the set-up men. Their job was to fix machines when they broke down. They had some big machines called Broaches that only the men could run because of the danger. There was also a guard on a high, closed-in platform, watching to make sure everything was okay. The paymaster was the General and he would come around in his uniform to give us our pays.

After I left the Springfield Armory, I went to work at the Fisk Rubber Plant in Chicopee, making patches for tanks and armory trucks. I also worked on the tubes that went inside the tires. The tires were not like they are today.

We were called Rosie the Riveter. I am very proud of the hard work I did. That was my part in the war effort, 60 years ago.

MY ASSEMBLYLINE EXTENDED FAMILY
by Marion Gene Crass Aulger
Whittier, California

Marion Aulger in the 1940's (left) and in 2004

I was 16 years old on a beach in Santa Monica, California, listening to the radio with a friend, when we heard that Pearl Harbor had been bombed. My father sent me to live in safety with my mother. Two years later, in 1943, I returned to California, determined to do my part for the war effort. I was hired by Douglas Aircraft in Santa Monica and trained to be a riveter on the bombers being built there.

To break the boredom of the fast, repetitious work, we once had a contest to see which team could buck and shoot the tail section of the plane the fastest, with no errors. The leadman shot and I bucked. I was inside the tail and could not see the shooter, and had to follow and keep up with the rivets he shot in. We came in first place! I was so proud of our success.

We had a wonderful group of people in our department. We went bowling as a group in the mornings, and later, about 20 of us took up ice skating. Most places stayed open 24/7 to accommodate the people who worked odd hours.

In 1944, I went to work at North American Aircraft in El Segundo, California. I continued to work as a riveter, but then I worked on twin-tail fighter planes. I made a new bunch of friends. On my twentieth birthday, the assembly line was stopped and they gave me a big pot luck party – right on the assembly line!

I made a lot of friends in my years as a "Rosie the Riveter" and I'm proud to have contributed my part to the war effort.

Marion with fellow workers at Douglas Aircraft in 1945

TELETYPIST ROSIE
by Betty Brill Updike
Sun City, Arizona

Betty Updike in the 1940's

In January, 1944, as a Wyoming high school senior, I had the opportunity to apply for training and employment with Western Union in California. I passed the necessary tests and, as an early graduate, was on my own at age 17.

One other girl traveled with me, and we became roommates during our training at Santa Cruz, California. I was fascinated with the operation of the teleprinter, typing messages on one machine, and retrieving them on another. We studied hard to learn Western Union's precise methods of messaging.

After graduation in March, I was sent to San Luis Obispo. The streets were teeming with our military troops.

Having just graduated from training school, I was assigned to most any station in the office, and I did work wherever and whenever I was needed.

I was just settling into a routine when I was sent to Camp Roberts as a relief operator. Camp Roberts, I was told, was the longest military base in the United States. The Western Union office was on one end of the base and my "room" was on the other end! I worked a triple-split shift, bussing back and forth.

After a few weeks, I was sent briefly to Oxnard, and later to Long Beach. The office was centrally located downtown, and usually packed with sailors. Besides the personal and business messages – some coded, which we handled on the main teleprinters – we had five or six tie-lines to military facilities – the Naval Hospital, Naval Air, Red Cross, and others. In addition, I was sent to north Long Beach as a relief operator/manager.

I was "frozen" to my job for the duration of WW II, but when our government needed teletypists at the Naval facility at Terminal Island, I applied and was accepted. I was hired for "ship-to-shore" communications and was looking forward to more training in that field when WW II ended.

THE ROSIE STORY OF SUSAN T. KING

by
Susan Emmaline Taylor King

Baltimore, Maryland

Susan Taylor King as she appeared on her Hampton Institute Student ID card for the 1944-45 year

    I was born on July 1, 1924 in Upper Tidewater, Virginia in the town of Kilmarnock. During the Depression, my family was just barely able to survive on my father's scant resources as a waterman in rural Virginia. Just prior to WW II, my family moved to Baltimore, Maryland, so that my father could earn $5.00 a day working at the shipyard. My family of seven traveled 150 miles by car to Baltimore. All the children entered schools in Baltimore. I entered Douglas High School.

    Six months after graduation, WW II began. I graduated in the academic curriculum; therefore, I had no skills for the world of work. My two friends and I entered riveting school because we had heard that there were a lot of jobs available. We attended riveting school on Washe Street in an old school building that no longer exists.

    Baltimore was a "top of the South or bottom of the

North" city. There were separate signs on all of the stores downtown, directing blacks to use one facility and whites to use another. Public schools were also segregated, so the riveting school was in a black neighborhood. Transportation, however, was not segregated.

When we finished riveting school in 1942, we were hired immediately at Eastern Aircraft on Broening Highway in the southeast section of Baltimore City. Work at Eastern Aircraft was completely integrated. All workers ate in the same cafeteria. There seemed to be a social or civil relationship between the black and white workers. I was a riveter who worked on the wings of aircraft. I assembled small parts that made up the wings, and a supervisor would come by with a magnifying glass to make sure that all of the parts were assembled correctly.

After the workday, we returned to our neighborhoods, churches, movies, clubs, and social activities. This was before the neighborhoods were integrated. We had the USO, where the soldiers came to dance and spend an evening in Baltimore. I became a pen pal to a few servicemen. After ten months of work at Eastern Aircraft, I decided to enter college. I felt strongly that there must be a way to help my community. I entered college and later received my Bachelor of Science and my Masters degrees from Morgan State University in Baltimore. My career continued after riveting, and I worked in the Baltimore City Public School System as a science teacher and a guidance counselor.

I am the widow of the late Dr. John Wesley King, who was a professor at Morgan State University. I am the mother of two daughters. One is the founder of the Sankofa Dance Theater and the other is a teacher. I am also the grandmother of seven and the great-grandmother of eight.

I am essentially a "peace" person. I consider all wars inhumane. We have a superior brain and technology, and humanity can best be served in peace.

LIBERATOR BOMBERS
by Lois Wolfe Richards Tretheway
Sun City West, Arizona

Lois Wolfe Tretheway in 1992 with one of the last
B-24 Liberator Bombers left flying

I was a calculator and operator during WW II. I tested the engines of the B-24 Liberator Bombers at the Buick plant in Melrose Park, Illinois, in 1942-43.

The engines were Pratt-Whitney #1830-94. Each engine was 1200 horsepower with a top speed of 275 miles per hour. The Liberator had four engines and served in all theaters of the war.

I worked the "swing shift" and the plant worked around the clock. I was 18 years old – we all had to grow up fast because our country was at WAR!!

In 1944, I married my hometown sweetheart, John Richards. He was in the Navy and we were sent to Port

Hueneme Point Mugu Naval Station in California. I worked in the office at PNAB, Pacific Naval Air Base.

John Richards passed away in Februrary, 1983. I married M. Trethewey in January, 1988. He passed away in December, 1995. At the age of 74, I moved to Sun City West, Arizona, along with other very busy seniors.

(Above) Two B-24 bombers leaving for a mission in 1943. (Right) Interior controls of a B-24 Liberator Bomber like those on which Lois Tretheway was calculator and operator.

A FAMILY FULL OF ROSIES
by Betty Pazdro
Rochester Hills, Michigan

(Left) Betty Pazdro in the 1940's, holding a picture of her husband, who was serving in Europe. (Right) In 2004, an article in The Detroit News *told about Betty, age 81, still working in her real estate office.*

    I worked at the Packard Motor Car Company in Detroit, Michigan, as a major inspector for airplane motor parts during 1943, 1944, and part of 1945. We worked from 7:30 p.m. to 6:00 a.m., Monday through Friday, and on Saturday from noon to 4:00 p.m. Women could only work 54 hours a week. My hourly wage was 98 cents per hour.

    I worked with my sister, Mary, and other girls who were ages 18 to 24. Several of our husbands were in the service. My husband was in Europe, beginning in England. My sister's husband was in Europe and had been in North Africa. Rita's husband was captured in Italy. Julia's husband was in the South Pacific. Lulu's husband was in Europe.

The other girls were single and helped keep up our spirits and morale.

No one had a car. However, we didn't have any problem getting around, since the buses and streetcars were always available.

We had several other family members who were "Rosies." My sister, Barbara, whose husband was in the Navy, worked at Continental Motors. My mom and my sister, Rose, worked in a defense plant as machinists.

When my brother, John, who was in the Navy in the south Pacific, and my brother-in-law, Matthew, came home on furlough, and my husband was home on a weekend pass, the family came together and my mom cooked and baked all their favorite dishes. Of course, meat, butter, and other foods were rationed, but we  all saved our ration stamps to use when our husbands and brother came home.

We hung silver star flags in our windows to show that our men were overseas. Thank God we didn't need to put gold stars in our windows, which meant the loss of a serviceman. They all came home safely.

I am now 81 and am still working as a real estate broker. I have no plans to retire. I love working with people that I work with, and when I place people in homes, they're like family to me. People ask me how I stay so active. I tell them that I take care of myself. I'm a health nut, I always have been. I also have a good outlook and don't dwell on the past.

MY WORK FOR THE RAILROAD
by Pauline Barker Booth
Oregon City, Oregon

(Left) Pauline Barker Booth in the 1940's.
(Right) Pauline handing up a message to the Hog Head at the front of a train.

I was working as a waitress during the war in Winslow, Arizona. I had two children, William Edward and Martha Leona, ages 4 and 2. My girlfriend was working for the railroad. She asked me to come and work with her, so I did.

The pay was okay and there was a place to live, rent-free. There were three girls to each station, and stations were ten miles apart. The station itself was an old diner car, with the office in front and an apartment in the back of the car. There were always two trailers on site and they were nice. Each girl had her own place to live. I thought it was a good deal for the kids and me.

I loved it at first, but we poor girls didn't know what we were in for. We were at the mercy of anything that came along. The office was all windows, and at night you didn't know who might be watching you. A lot of people knew we were out there by ourselves. I was scared all the time.

I took the night shift because I could be with the kids all day. While the kids were in bed, I would walk a few feet to the office. I could see the trailer out the window.

The train orders were given to us by a dispatcher over the phone, and we had to write out what he said and hand that message up on a stick to the engineer (called the Hog Head) at the head of the train, then stay there by that train in the dead of night to hand the same message up to the breakman in the caboose. Some of the girls were crushed to death under the wheels of the train while doing this. We also had to stop a lot of trains and put them in the siding so another train could go on. To keep them from a head-on crash, we had to throw a switch to make the train go into the siding. It wasn't easy to do – a switch took all the strength I had.

One night the dispatcher called and said there was a train on its way that had missed his message at the last station, and that I was to head him into the siding. I would have to run as fast as I could to meet the train about a mile away, or there would be one big wreck with another train and some lives would be taken, because the other train was a passenger train.

I told the dispatcher I couldn't do it, I was too frightened. He told me that the lives lost would forever be with me and that I *could* do it. So I took myself out of the office with one last look at my trailer and my kids sleeping. I thought I might never see them again.

I had my lantern and flares to break open. I did make it just in time to get the train into the siding, then we saw the lights of the passenger train coming. I couldn't believe I did it. The men on the train couldn't believe it, either. They all gave me a hand, and said what a brave girl I was, but I didn't feel very brave. I was the talk of the town in that small railroad town of Seligman, Arizona.

INDEX

of names and places of work

A

A & R Aerial Repair, 148
Aeroproducts Aviation, 172
Aircraft carrier, 34
Alameda Air Field, 108
Anderson Airplane School, 121
Anderson, Velora L. S. S., 165
Angell, Jan ,11
Armstrong, Helen Ensey, 15
Ash, LaPriel Frandsen, 53
Athens Shipyard, 65
Atomic bomb, 5, 178
Aulger, Marion Gene, 197

B

B-17 airplane, 16, 42, 29, 35, 71, 93, 96, 126, 157, 182
B-24 airplane, 14, 39, 42, 43, 93, 160, 188, 203
B-25 airplane, 93
B-26 airplane, 60,121,173,175
B-29 airplane, 16, 67, 75, 82, 86, 93, 138, 144, 160, 168, 170, 180, 182, 188, 192
B-49 airplane, 108
B-52 airplane, 168
Barrett, Joyce Pistole, 89
Beard, Marie Reichert, 119
Beech Aircraft, 167, 186
Belcher, Hazel Mae, 191
Berger Aircraft, 123
Berry, Dena Mai Peach, 121
Bechtel McCombs Parsons Airplane Modification Plant, 20, 67, 144, 188

Black Cats, 1
Blackler, Eileen Trout, 129
Blume, Odean Gregg, 101
Boeing, 11, 16, 35, 75, 77, 87, 135, 137, 145, 168, 170, 179, 181
Booth, Pauline Barker, 207
Brady, Virginia Ellis, 37
Bremerton Naval Shipyards, 150
Brookley Field, 79
Brooks, Elizabeth Betterley,13
Buckingham Air Force Base, 121
Buick, 203
Bumgardner, Charlotte, 181
Burkhardt, Joseph, Jr., 69
Burkhardt, Mae, 69

C

C-47 airplane, 38, 80, 83, 91, 111, 141
C-Master, 133
Cadet Nursing, 22
California Shipyard, 56
Carnegie-Illinois Steel, 110
Camp Roberts, 200
Carter, Frances Tunnell, 187
Cessna, 143, 167
Chanute Air Force Base, 4
Chason, Jane Headrick, 61
Childress Army Air Force Base, 89
China Lake Navy Base, 30
Chrysler Motors, 21, 105
Clayberger, Joan Sargent, 189
Collier, Frankie Jane L,, 83

Commercial Iron Works, 130
Consolidated Aircraft, 70, 161
Curtiss Wright, 11, 113, 115, 128

D

Dalzell, Louise Hessek, 109
Danly Machine Specialties, 8
Dixie Manufacturing Company, 18
Dodge Forge Plant, 105
Doebbeling, Anne Lewis, 75
Domenick, Mary Lou F., 27
Donohue, Gladys Owenby, 177
Douglas Aircraft, 38, 43, 83, 91, 95, 101, 111, 141, 197
Du Lac, Mary Maslonka, 15

E

Easley, Iva Jean Ellis, 37
Eastern Aircraft, 163, 176, 202
Enola Gay, 112, 180, 192

F

Felton, Patricia J., 57
Field, Florence Steere, 193
Firestone, 1
Fisk Rubber Plant, 196
Fix, Carolyn E., 155
Food Machinery Corporation, 3
Fortner, Ella M. Tauzin, 69, 161
Fox, Marian, 99
Fox, Vera M., 133
Fredricksen, Freddella Iverson, 49

G

G & H Manufacturing Co., 135
GLF Petroleum Company, 65

Gates Rubber Plant, 167
General Motors, 163
Glenn L. Martin Aircraft, 59, 103, 119, 133, 173, 175
Goodyear, 25
Gowan Air Force Base, 41
Grant, Kate, 31

H

Hamilton, Dorine Smith, 87
Hamilton, Loraine Sublett, 185
Hanke, Lanelle, 161
Harless Mattress Company, 143
Harper, Hazel Owenby, 5
Hasty, Vernelle Brown, 143
Hell Diver, 128
Hickam Field, 57, 93
Higgins Industries Shipyard, 34
Highsmith, Donna Carpenter, 93
Hill, Irene M., 91
Hoaglund, Mary Hairston, 159
Hockensmith Company, 27
Hoines, Pansy Ethelyn Dunkle, 149
Hrabec, Joyce, 7
Hudson Motor Car Company, 21

I-J

Irvin, Ruth McEhaney, 47
Jayme, Gladys Marley, 95
John Mansville Roofing Co., 32
Johnson, Ann Ramirez, 9
Johnson, Anna L., 167
Jones, Velores McLean, 39

K

Kaiser Shipyards, 9, 33, 131, 146
Kessler, Marianne Mueller, 151

King, Susan T., 201
Konieczny, Anna Maslonka, 105

L

Landry, Barbara Burkhardt, 69
Lane, Florence E. Wilkinson, 183
Leuck, Eleanor Clyden, 3
Lears Aviation, 171
Levitas, Jean Rubin Meyers, 163
Lewis, Dorothy Case, 17, 19
Lewis, Nell Case Morgan, 19
Liberty Ship, 31, 34, 56, 99, 157
Lockheed Aircraft Corporation, 29, 50, 72, 78, 139, 193
Logan, Marion E. Hoines, 147, 149
Lorette, Cleo Evans, 43
Lund, Jean L. Kowalski, 169

M

Maritime Commission, 55
Marmon Products, 186
Martin, Dorothy Hopper, 77
Matheny, Velma M., 153
McClend Field, 107
McCloskey's Shipbuilding, 23
McDaniel, Lela Morlan, 113
McDonnell Douglas Aircraft, 38, 56, 96, 113, 157
McMasters, Margot Bersos, 35
Missouri Pacific Railroad, 151
Mock, Rozella Petersen, 41
Morrissette, Gloria Wassung, 195
Morton Aircraft, 71
Mossman Company, 64
Murray Corporation, 39, 126
Myrick, Mabel Wolford, 97

N

Nakashima, Signe Olson, 29
National Youth Administration (NYA), 81, 86, 113, 155, 173
Naval Gun Factory, 74
Nichols, Mary Crapster, 59
Nichols, Nora E. Petrie Willis, 103
Nikolaisen, Polly, 139
Nist, Joan Stidham, 63
Norick, Madalynne King, 111
North American Aircraft, 198

O

Oak Ridge, Tennessee, 5, 178
O'Quinn, Elaine Smith, 137
Oregon Shipyards, 99, 189

P

P-38 airplane, 29, 72, 82, 140, 160, 193
PBM-3 aircraft, 119, 133
PBY5a aircraft, 70, 162
PV-2 aircraft, 29
Pacific Naval Air Base, 204
Packard Motor Car Company, 205
Paddock, Josephine Binelli, 65
Page Field, 122
Patterson Air Field, 86
Payant, Elizabeth A., 21
Pazdro, Betty, 205
Pearl Harbor, 17, 25, 49, 51, 63, 71, 79, 83, 95, 109, 115, 129, 131, 165, 171, 183, 195
Pearson, Eleanor L., 33
Pentagon, 97
Philley, Dora Bea Cox, 157
Plymouth plant, 106
Posko, Theresa Dypsky, 175

Pratt Whitney Aircraft, 72
Pringle, Nellie Rains, 73
Puget Sound Sheet Metal, 170
Putnam, Lola M. Bates, 107

Q-R

Richmond Shipyards, 31
Riley, Caroline, 135
Robins Air Force Base, 82
Rojas, Manuela A., 45
Roosevelt, Eleanor, 34, 173
Roosevelt, Franklin Delano (FDR), 3, 25, 33, 78, 92, 129, 172, 174
Ryan, Lena England, 67

S

Salerno, Jeanette, 135
Sargent, Mildred Crow, 127
Savage Arms Company, 155
Savannah Shipyard, 61
Seattle Port, 53
Sedwick, Ruth Slack, 115
Sellers, Ora Caroline L., 173
Shaffer, Fannie Eleanor, 123
Sherrow, Kathleen, 71
Solar and Ryan Aircraft, 56
Springfield Armony, 195
Smith, Darlene P. DeMars, 179
Spruce Goose, 174
St. Louis Ordnance Plant, 165
Stanley, Lessie Hendon, 1
Stevenson, Phillys Janet, 157
Stoutamire, Mary Taliaferro, 81
Superior Mold & Iron Co., 27

T

Taylor, Ginny, 55
Thomas, Carrie H., 141

Tinker Air Force Base, 57, 84, 91, 93, 112, 141, 148, 191
Tinker, June Midkiff, 85
Tretheway, Lois Wolfe, 203
Tringe, Mary, 117
Turner, Helen M., 131
Turney, Roxie Ott, 51

U

Updike, Betty Brill, 199
United Airlines, 71
U. S. Cartridge Company, 165
U. S. Engineers, 109
U. S. Steel, 110
USO, 8, 25, 130, 136, 166, 172, 188

V

Van Alstine, Marjorie A., 145
Van Betten, Patricia Tringe, 117
Van Ralte Hosiery, 177

W

War Department, 44, 97
War Housing Office, 59
War Training Center, 15
Wheeler Field, 63
Wilkins, Frances Smith, 79
Willow Run Bomber Plant, 39
Woodall Industries, 127
Woodruff, Easter Jones, 23

X-Y-Z

Yanacek, Mescal P., 25
Young, Donna Belcher, 191
Zimmerman, Maxine, 171
Zumblin, Patricia, 105

AMERICAN ROSIE THE RIVETER ASSOCIATION ®

Founded 1998

PURPOSE:

To recognize and preserve the history and legacy of working women, including volunteer women, during World War II; to promote cooperation and fellowship among such members and their descendants; and to further the advancement of patriotic ideals, excellence in the work place, and loyalty to the United States of America.

WHO MAY BELONG?

Women whose work during 1941-1945 was designed to contribute to the war effort (including women who did volunteer work) and their female descendants are eligible for active membership. Spouses and male descendants may become auxiliary members. Women who performed the work are known as **Rosies**. Their female descendants are **Rosebuds**. Male auxiliary members are known as **Rivets**. Those who have no record of whether their mother or grandmother worked during the war, but who would like to uphold the purpose of the organization may join as **Rosebud Partners** or **Rivet Partners**. Women who currently work or have retired from a job that prior to World War II was considered "man's work" may join as **21st Century Rosies**.

Qualifying work for Rosies may consist of:

1. Employment of any sort in an industry or government agency directly related to the war effort, **or**

2. Employment, including self-employment (such as farming), in a capacity usually held by a man, thus releasing the man for military duty, **or**

3. Participation on a sustained basis in one or more volunteer activities related to the war effort.

Rosebuds and Rivets are eligible for membership, regardless of whether their Rosie is living or deceased, and whether or not the Rosie was a member of the Association. For a membership application or to find more information, visit our Web site at www.rosietheriveter.net.

Enjoy all of these historical books published by the American Rosie the Riveter Association®!

103 Rosie the Riveter Stories

Rosie the Riveter Celebration Cookbook

104 More Rosie the Riveter Stories

Rosie Romances and Other Rosie the Riveter Stories

Copies of all of these books may be ordered from:
    ARRA Books
    P.O. Box 188
    Kimberly, AL 35091

For more information, visit www.rosietheriveter.net.

True stories written by the Rosies themselves!